MW01634538

Test of FAITH

Winemakers say that the finest wines are made from grapes whose mother vine makes her way through the worst soil -- pushing persistent roots through rocks, gravel, weaving around over and through the most inhospitable environments. These vines produce the tastiest grapes, highly prized for their hard won quality. The worse the soil conditions, it is said, the finer the grapes.

Test of FAITH

Hope, Courage and the Prison Experience

Eva

Evelyn

Hanks

Canadian Scholars' Press   Toronto   2000

Test of Faith: Hope, Courage and the Prison Experience
by Eva Evelyn Hanks

First published in 2000 by
Canadian Scholars' Press Inc.
180 Bloor Street West, Suite 1202
Toronto, Ontario
M5S 2V6
www.cspi.org

Copyright © 2000 by Eva Evelyn Hanks and Canadian Scholars' Press. All rights reserved. No part of this publication may be photocopied, reproduced, stored in a retrieval system, or transmitted, in any form or by any means, electronic, mechanical or otherwise, without the written permission of Canadian Scholars' Press, except for brief passages quoted for review purposes.

Every reasonable effort has been made to identify copyright holders. Canadian Scholars' Press would be pleased to have any errors or omissions brought to its attention.

CSPI acknowledges the financial support of the Government of Canada through the Book Publishing Industry Development Programme for our publishing activities.

Canadian Cataloguing in Publication Data

Hanks, Eva Evelyn, 1957-
      Test of faith : hope, courage and the prison experience

ISBN 1-55130-176-8

1. Hanks, Eva Evelyn, 1957-   —Diaries. 2. Prisoners – Ontario.
3. Prisons – Ontario. 4. Prisoners' spouses – Ontario – Diaries. I. Title.

HV9509.O5H36 2000   365'.6'092   C00-930934-9

Managing Editor: Ruth Bradley-St-Cyr
Marketing Manager: Susan Cuk
Interior and cover design: Amy Seagram

00 01 02 03 04 05 06 6 5 4 3 2 1

Printed and bound in Canada by AGMV Marquis

Acknowledgements

I wish to acknowledge Dr. Ruth Morris, founder of Rittenhouse, for her encouragement, kindness and enormous help in reading and promoting the manuscript; Maria Karajovanova, for her friendship, which defies description, (as she herself does); Giselle Dias, Michelle Sauve, Ann Lay and the many other friends, especially those I have met through JustUs and Rittenhouse, who have supported me through all of the troubles, heartaches and joys that this story enfolds; Jack Wayne, publisher of Canadian Scholars' Press, who believes in the importance of the truth and who delighted me by actually enjoying the book!; and Ruth Bradley-St-Cyr, Managing Editor, whose respect for the integrity of the original manuscript was exceptional.

Dedicated to Ted, with all my love

Introduction

*C*old, wet, mixed rain and slushy snow—we'd had it all winter so far. I started
to cry already before I even stood there in front of it, not believing, grey stone
and beautiful, a sleeping silent cobra keeping hate and secret horrors hidden from
the casual passer-by. A few others stood waiting, I passed them without looking. A
massive iron door it didn't even budge when I pulled. Jumped, I startled, when the
voice crackled, the speaker beside the door I didn't see at first.
"Yes, ma'am, what's your business here?"
I must have been their entertainment. A newcomer. Deer in the headlights.
"I'm... I'm... uh... here for a visit. M-my-my..."
"Visiting's not til 9:30 a.m." the speaker dead again and I standing, staring
through amber glass barely making out their shapes behind it. I curled into the
cobra's coils for cold comfort against the greyness of the day, this moment that I
still waited to wake up from some awful dream and shake it off stumbling to the
bathroom saying, "Oh my gawd, what a horrible..."
I was surely their entertainment that morning.

9:31 ticked off and the door buzzed a low growl. The cobra's jaws unhinged,
I fumbled with my I.D. in line. A sign, I almost tripped over it but didn't read
it, saying "Take a number" so like an idiot I instead walked straight into the
waiting area. Another one, she told me "You have to take a number." I stared
again like a lunatic, she stuck out her chin pointing with it to the stack of
numbers on a stand stuck to the wall. Like I was in the bad dream I walked
back to the numbers, and took one, that were past ten already 'cause they'd
been before and I was the only newcomer so far.

I gripped the hard meat market number, and traced the number eleven and walked dream-hazed back to sit on the wooden bench beside the one who had been kind, only yet I didn't recognize it was a kindness she'd done. I cried again, only still, my shoulders shaking and I didn't care but still I felt embarrassed red, thank gawd they're all women they have sons and lovers.

They all feel bad and silent on me only I don't recognize the carved out silence yet as compassion amongst comrades. One of them is telling her story and all I hear is my head saying, "what will I tell my parents" as if I needed to tell them anything I hadn't seen them in a year already what would they need to hear from me. "what will I tell my parents," a woman of 38 years, teenagers of my own, divorced and Catholic left the church then married again to no money no future, what did I need to tell them? But it was all that kept coming and the tears kept coming and the others talked amongst themselves, their silence at me a shield against the hurt that I didn't see until much later, when I was the old hand.

"Eleven" he called and I cowered at the window while he asked the questions, sick in my stomach when my mouth made his name out loud, still not believing it's true, and still I'm crying. Behind the glass blue uniform, looked out at me and then acted like he's got a heart and so looked past my face like the tears weren't there. He didn't hassle the I.D. on me and he said with some kindness, which I recognized then, "when your number is called you go to the back and they'll let you in to see him."

I squeezed a look through to the back where you couldn't see much but I made out a counter and a wall of glass all around a dark hole inside which they waited their turn, much like us out there in the lighted hole. We had benches where we were, they were standing. There were phones-like, not real like a dialling one or touch tone, but just receivers and when you got up to it you could see them clearly through the smudgy glass all covered in greasy nose and fingerprints and last week's slimy kisses.

Two hours waiting and number eleven was called to the telephone counter. Another low growling door and I pulled it and it opened and I walked through it like the looking glass only it was more weird and twisted even than Alice's was 'cause this one was real and would never let me out.

I cried the whole time, "why" was everything I could only say and crying the whole time.

He was sad and so sorry only what could he say he said little only, "Sorry... I never meant..." and it was over, ten minutes was up and my two hours wait was disappeared in ten minutes of crying over and over again, "why." "I love you" we both said.

Like a miracle it was only the very next day and I knew then not to pull on the door but just to wait in line for the meat market number and show the I.D. and without even a tear I said his name and sat to wait my two hours on the wooden bench. I did it every Saturday and Sunday and my ten minutes time after two hours waiting became ritual, a waited-all-week for moment where even the smudgy glass didn't bother as much.

Weeks rolled into months and now they had plants in the room where we waited on wooden benches, they added some benches too and I'm hip to the microphones hidden in the plants and so I shoot the breeze with his visiting friend and we said no words like "charges" or "guilty" or "murder." These are bad words that get them killed inside if they are overheard out in the planty room.

A deal was made in offices where people do those things and we don't know if the deal is good but it gets him out of there and onto hard time, which at least counts. We thought that it was touching, holding, finally embracing, six months making a glass sandwich but the glass is there again and the guards this place are growlier, hearts that got ruined in forever black rain. These ones don't care their meanness shows as long as they make you know they own him and you and "who do you think you are" he growled at me and I raged inside and said "FuckyouFuckyouFuckyou" in silence. Goddam I know who I am you bastard, it's *you* who lost *you* along the way. At least it's only seven years for us in this hell, and better for sucking in our pride with bastards like you to smile and kiss your ass at, but you, you're here forever and no life left. Go home to frigid wives that hate your breath stink and you think you're somebody.

And when it came time and they said that I could, I got to the big house real early, long before the gate house was awake and open and only the tower could see me. And so I got in line the first and I got my visit, six hours drive and two hours visit making the glass sandwich but every laugh and our hands together on the glass is worth it. It's long and longer before the glass is gone.

And now at last the visit is glassless, just as long as our feet stay on the ground with shoes kept on and "no intertwining of limbs" but arms around each other holding like forever and all the black Millhaven past and Toronto Jail is like a story overheard. It's only us and 50 other people are not there in the room around us, and soon this too will be a past story, history past long since. The love is forever and tested true it will come through. We wait and the story isn't over.

❖

Wine *makers say that the finest wines are made from grapes whose mother vine makes her way through the worst soil—pushing persistent woody roots through rocks, gravel, weaving around over and through the most inhospitable environments. These vines produce the tastiest grapes, highly prized for their hard won quality. The worse the soil conditions, it is said, the finer the grape.*

I take some comfort in the thought. Dubious honour, though, for the grape, to have its essence, its life-blood distilled only to live on in the coveted bottles buried deep in some rich man's cellar.

M's Chapter One

We left by the side door of the bank, right on schedule, keeping our heads down, careful not to make eye contact with anyone. We walked quickly across L_____ Avenue towards the laneway in back of the bank across the street. We were both wearing X-large coveralls that we had split at the seams and sewn Velcro into so they could be stripped off in a second. I had my hand on the .44 cal. gun in my right-hand pocket, which hung loose, covering my hand and the gun.

"There they go!" I heard someone shout, just as we neared the shadowed lip of the laneway.

My grip on the gun tightened as I released the safety catch.

"Don't look up." I said in a low monotone to S. who was right on my heels and panting with the urge to run. The adrenaline was pumping wildly now, but I felt as calm as though I was born to this; we started a quick jog just as we rounded the corner of the other bank and we headed straight down the laneway to where the car was waiting, engine running. It was there as planned, on our left-hand side, backed into a concealed corner that no one would see if they looked down the laneway. The headlights were on and I could see S's silhouette emerge as he stepped into their halo.

It was at that precise moment that I knew that something was about to go very wrong.

It was 6.5 seconds getting from the door of the bank to the car, as previously timed, through many rehearsals. In performance, it was 6.5 seconds that lasted as many years.

I heard the hum of the engine and a "clunk" as D. put it into drive. I stopped short and grabbed S's coveralls at the back of the neck and ripped them off him in one pull as he passed me. He didn't lose a step. I threw the coveralls through the open car door into the back seat and barked at S. to throw them into the hockey bag that had been placed in the back seat.

All the "equipment" was to go into this bag—money, gun, disguises, everything. That bag was scheduled to be removed from the car in 45 seconds. The plan was, as we headed out of the laneway to the east and turned south, S. would get out of the car and throw this bag into the trunk of car number two, then throw the key in after it. Then he'd walk north to Queen St., an innocent bystander.

I slammed the back door of the car and flung open the front passengers' door. Just as I threw my left leg into the car, I saw a shadow jump out into the glare of the headlights and heard the scream, "Freeze!"

That's exactly what we did. He was standing about two feet in front of the car, a plain-clothes cop and at first he seemed to not know what else to do or say. The lights from the car were shining right in his face and we were all frozen. His hand was shaking so hard he had to put his other hand over it just to keep it still. It shook anyway and his both hands not keeping the gun from shaking gave him away. I knew all he was thinking right now was how the hell he was going to get out of this and how come it wasn't like on T.V. and what if his gun went off on its own and all the paperwork and days of embarrassing questions and blood on the sidewalk—maybe his own.

My left arm was still on top of the car and my right hand was at my side. He couldn't see as I slipped my right hand into the baggy coverall pocket and took a firm grip again, on the .44. I had it pointed right at him and he didn't even know it. He couldn't see my hand, couldn't see me except as a shadow behind the blaze of the headlights.

He screamed at me to get my hands where he could see them. When I failed to obey he seemed to get more nervous and his voice rose higher as he shrieked the order again. "Get your fucking hands up!!" and it came out in a split scream, like his voice had cracked in two and the higher note it took was where he really lived, in that moment.

I thought for sure D. would hit him with the car; it was still in drive, all he had to do was to hit the gas and knock him down. And I thought for sure he would and I waited for it. I still didn't raise my hands.

The cop was young and he was really scared now. He was wishing like hell that he hadn't tried to be a hero tonight. I must have looked like the grim reaper staring out through the darkness, spreading icy fingers around his future. He didn't need to see my eyes to know I was looking straight at him, right in his eyes, right through him. And he could feel me thinking.

He had been standing there, trying to hold the gun still for about 20 seconds now and his voice kept splintering and rising, higher and more panicky each time he whined, "Get your fucking hands up, get them up, hands up, UP! UP! UP! I can't see your hands..." he was almost moaning. I thought he might even start screaming "*Please*," but he didn't.

I turned my head slowly to the left and looked down into the car at S. who was laying on the floor in the back seat trying to stuff the bag under the front seat. He later told me that he was trying to jam it in front of himself in case shots came through the car. D. sat stone still in the driver's seat like he was in a trance or a coma, just staring at the cop standing there in the headlights of the car, that was *still* in drive, his foot frozen on the brake.

I looked back at the cop and his hands were shaking so hard now, I thought for sure he would drop the gun—or shoot me in the face. He began waving the gun back and forth at me and the driver, still babbling, his voice a hoarse screech now, fingernails on a chalkboard.

I realized by this time that D. wasn't going to wake up from his state of suspended animation. He didn't have the balls to hit the cop with the car and the cop didn't have the balls to pull the trigger. S. didn't have the balls to even lift his head from where he lay crouched down into the floor of the back seat to see what the fuck was actually going on. I was considering options. Options, I realized with a shock, that I had never considered before.

I could hear sirens from the uniform cops getting closer now and I knew I was down to seconds to make a choice before it was made for me. I could shoot the cop—I had the gun pointed straight at him and that .44 magnum would go through the car frame, through him and his vest if he was wearing one, and probably right on through the brick wall behind him.

I measured the distance to freedom in parts of a second, less than 1/4 of a second to pull the trigger and I'd have the cop out of the way; if D. was still shitting his pants and couldn't drive, I could shoot him in another 1/2 second and push him out of the car with enough seconds left to drive away before the siren I heard in the distance could even get a good make on the car or the plate.

But then I'd have to shoot S. too, it would have to be all of them. It was a choice that hadn't occurred to me. I remembered I promised myself that I would never let anyone get hurt.

The cop still held the gun with both hands and while he stood there and shouted with shaking arms stretched out in front of him, a million thoughts crossed my mind and one so bizarre I might have laughed out loud and maybe I did without knowing it. What if he pissed his pants, would I even be able to stop laughing long enough to seize the moment and run?

Did cops in Toronto really shoot people or did they only fantasize their heroism, falling asleep with sugar-plum visions of their own stardom on "Cops," like their big brothers in the big, bad U.S. of A.; the swaggering heroes they could never quite be like but they could strut and use words like "perp" and "take-down" that they learned from slick cop shows that imitated life, and then they'd feel more like them, like those "real cops."

All of this passed through my head in another fraction of a second and I deliberated one more time, shoot the cop or not? I thought of how it would be to tell my kids I had shot a cop and I don't think it was that thought that made up my mind but a door shut somewhere in my head and I realized that shooting him, or anyone, was not an option I could choose.

I could try to throw the gun away to not get busted with it. But if the cop saw my hand come up with the gun, if he could see even just an outline of it, for sure he'd shoot me in the head. I could run. It would mean going right by him under the dim lights of the laneway—dim but bright enough to let him get a good shot at my back. My last option was to put my hands up.

That's when I spoke to him for the first time. "Hey bud, I'm going to put my hands up nice and slow. Just relax, nothing bad is going to happen." I said it calmly, like this was something I did every day, not at all like I was writing the script as we went. I let go of the gun and eased my hand out of my pocket; I spoke in a soft, low voice, trying to calm him down—he was completely frantic by now. I couldn't understand a word he was saying anymore.

"Okay, pal, here we go. Easy, easy, easy," I was saying quietly, as I carefully put both hands behind my head. I walked to the other side of the car door in his full, clear view for the first time, and lay on the ground with my hands behind my head.

He continued shouting, though the shrillness in his voice had begun to subside, ordering the others out of the car and on the ground. S. leapt from the floor of the car in a flash and lay with his face buried in the pavement, both hands clenched white behind his head. D. was still in a trance behind the wheel, staring at the cop who kept yelling "Get your hands up!" until he did.

"Get out of the car!" he screamed, his voice getting bolder with the two of us already subdued in front of him.

"I can't!" D. yelled back. "The car's in drive. It'll hit you."

"Get out! Get out! Get the fuck out!" he kept yelling.

I was still hoping D. would hit the gas and send the cop flying and I was ready to spring for the open door of the car if he did. But instead, D. suddenly moved his right hand down and put the car into park. He was lucky the cop didn't think he was going for a gun and shoot him. Maybe the cop couldn't shoot him. Or anyone. I still had the .44, safety off, in my right-hand pocket and he didn't know it. It would be over so fast, he'd never even know what hit him.

By the time the cruisers screamed into the laneway, with at least 15 uniformed cops pouring out of them, we were all face down in front of the car. Two of the uniforms yelled, "We got this one!" as one of them jumped and threw both knees into my back even while I was lying stone still on the ground. The other one kicked me in the back of the head and stepped on the back of my neck while the first one cuffed me. I said, "Hey, relax. You got me already, for fuck sakes." The second cop kicked me in the head again and I shut up.

I thought of how he'd go home tonight and play it out for all his pals and he'd be a hero in his kids wide eyes as he told them the story of how he arrested a notorious bank-robber. And then his wife would call all of her friends and her sisters and agonize to them about how terrifying it was to sit at home knowing he was out there chasing bad guys; but secretly the badge inside her shone brilliant and she would keep this one going for months at least, and maybe she would even sleep with him tonight and fake it, after all he *was* a hero.

I was looking out of the corner of my eye at the young plain-clothes cop who was doing that thing that kids do with their arm bent and pulling their fist down and saying "Yes!" He looked like an 8-year old who just scored his first goal. He acted so cool, so tough, his voice was hard and even.

That's when I said, very quietly, not threatening, "I have a gun in my right-hand pocket," I had purposely waited until I was "secured" to tell them I had a gun so they wouldn't all freak on me. But they did anyway, "He's got a gun! Jeezus, he's got a gun!" I was laying on my stomach, head pressed to one side on the pavement and my hands were cuffed behind my back. Two fat cops were still holding me down but they had to put shotguns to my head anyway, until they got the gun out of my pocket.

"Holy *fuck*, a .44," one of them said.

They grabbed my hair trying to pull me to my feet but it was too short to get a firm grip and I tried to stand, slowly so as not to alarm them. Before I could get onto my knees they jerked me straight up from the ground by the handcuffs, almost dislocating both my shoulders. It was my first chance to look eye to eye at the young cop.

"Safety?!" he asked, not taking his eyes off mine.

"Off," the uniform said, "and fully loaded."

I knew that he understood then that the only reason he was still alive was that I chose not to kill him. The boyish glee and gloating grin suddenly disappeared. I thought I could see a little wet spot appearing at his crotch and a thin trail of steam rising.

The uniform walked over to him to show him the gun but his eyes were still locked on mine. He didn't look at the other cop or the gun.

They shoved us into the back seats of two different cruisers and played good cop bad cop all the way to the station. I said nothing. I remember meditating in the cruiser on the way to 55 Division, sitting absolutely still with my eyes closed, numbing my body and trying to slow my heart rate just in case they took a few more cheap shots at me. It was going to be a long night.

When we got to the station I could see S. had been crying though he hung his head and tried to hide his face from me. I could smell his fear from the other room while they questioned us both. I didn't have a lawyer to call and it only struck me then how bizarre it was that the thought of getting caught had never once occurred to me. *Never once.*

It was still a thick fog I was thinking through but that one thought came through crystal clear. No phone call to make. There was a weird comfort in the anonymity of it.

W's Chapter One

I spent the weekend writing, some good material too, I was pleased with it. It felt good, even though underneath was the constant current of anxiety, waiting for the phone to ring, wondering what the silence was about this time.

We were growing apart, I knew it, but I allowed it, resigned to let it simply take its course this time. I had my own life, I was back on my feet, working and writing whenever I could find the time. He was doing his thing —whatever that was, I was never clear—and he was constantly disappearing for days at a time. The thought had occurred to me that he was maybe seeing someone else, and it hurt when it pierced through, like a bee-sting, and then, the same way, the sudden pain subsided and just a steady, achy throb was left behind.

I could live with it. This time if it didn't work, I was definitely out of it. We had tried too many times. It hurt me—the idea of being without him, of the dreams not ever becoming real. But it was different this time. I was different. I had become my own hero and I knew that I would survive anything. Even the threat of "losing my mind," so long a hungry hound at my heels, could not catch up to me now. I had played all the parts—the maiden in distress, the conquering hero, I had even played my own dragon, though there were enough eager dragons out there auditioning for the part. And I had survived them all.

The phone hadn't rung all weekend and its silence didn't disturb my writing. That couldn't have happened two years ago. I would have been frantic, pacing or maybe immobilized and gone to bed for two days. This time I delighted in my own company, happy to be writing again. Happy to see the words appear on the screen so effortlessly that they seemed to arrive there on their own.

After two days I needed a break from the keyboard so I went out for a coffee. Out of character, but needing some mindless escape I grabbed a newspaper and brought it home. The coffee was hot and good and I simply sat and sipped for awhile before I began leafing idly through pages of political grumbling and grisly accident reports and other mediocre ramblings that passed for news.

It's so strange, isn't it, how in a full page of newsprint one little word or phrase or name can just leap out like it's written in neon. That's how it happened that morning. Without warning his full name suddenly appeared, struck me full in the face, burned itself into my eyes. First I felt the flash of shock and then a thin flame of disbelief that suddenly roared into a full fire of horror. My hand shook and the coffee scalded my skin and spilled all over the page and still there it was. *Bank Robbers Arrested* and his name, spelled out in full, it was not a name that you ever heard twice, it had to be him. I read it over and over, simply not believing. I threw the paper across the room and ran to a mirror and pinched my face, my arms, it was real, no—God it was only a nightmare, I would wake up now, any minute.

I ran and picked up the paper again, read it again, and again. His name, his name, my god, his age, "no fixed address," why had he said that. Of course, he wouldn't have given my name or address. It was him. It was really him. Why wasn't I waking up yet. My god, this is real, this can't be. I paced like a crazed animal, *What to do, what to do. Where do they take them. How do I see him. MY GOD, it's really true. How could he, how could he?!* The dry sobs started then and I heard myself scream out loud, NO! No crying. No crying!

The dragon was at the door, great flames rising, its laughter echoing my every nightmare.

M's Chapter Two

It was impossible to sleep. The lights stayed on in this place day and night, bright lights shining in your face, 24/7. It was cold enough to see my breath and the jailhouse coveralls and shoes were soaked with the water from overflowing toilets that had been flooding the cells constantly since I got there. The mattress they gave me wasn't a full two inches deep at its thickest and the floor had been flooded at least a dozen times that day. What was left of my "bedding" was soaked through but it served to cover the filthy floor, strewn with cigarette butts, tight little wads of toilet paper and upturned corpses of cockroaches.

The toilets were being deliberately clogged by inmates on the second floor; they were stuffing sheets and towels into them, causing floods to protest the 24-hour lockdown that had started the day before, when the guards had voted to strike.

I was housed in 1-C in the Toronto Don Jail, "Reception." I overheard one of the others say that usually you are kept on 1-C for only a day and then moved to another cell-block to await your hearing. But because of the "zero movement" policy during the strike, I was stuck here until the strike was over, however long that might take. No sheets, no underwear, no socks, no T-shirt. Only the smelly coveralls and the mattress that had about fifteen years of every bodily fluid imaginable permanently soaked into it, obviously never cleaned. I wouldn't have let my dog sleep on that thing. But I lay there on it, listening and thinking.

The cell had two bunks but with the strike, they were throwing three of us into every cell in 1-C. When you put a mattress on the floor, it stretched from the bars to the just under the toilet bowl. You only had two choices as to which way to point your head, but towards the bars exposed my head to the breeze that came in. With no blanket, my clothing soaked and the 50 degree temperature, I finally got too cold and so I turned around and lay with my head by the toilet. It stank like hell, but I could smell it anyway and I just wanted to get my head away from the bars and that cold breeze.

The lights never go out and they felt like torture after awhile, but they're built into steel fixtures with some kind of Plexiglas covering them, so they can't be smashed. In spite of the lights and the cold, I must have dozed off for a minute and that was when I woke up to the splattering and spraying in my face.

My first waking thought was that the toilet had backed up again. I sprang up with a jolt and it felt like I'd hit a brick wall when I banged my head straight into his leg. He was standing right over me, straddling my head and the toilet bowl; he missed the bowl, hit the seat and the piss went splashing right into my face.

"You fucking asshole!" I yelled. I jumped to my feet and smashed my leg on the steel stool fastened to the wall. My eyes were flashing murder when the guy's cell partner slid down off his bunk and stood on the mattress in front of me. "What the fuck's up? What's your fuckin' problem?" he screamed, his face inches away from mine. I was in a blind rage, not thinking or even caring about getting myself killed in this place. The guard's keys jangled as he came towards the cell to investigate. He stood in the corridor, outside the door of the cage, coffee in hand. I told the guard to "get me the fuck outta here before I kill someone," which I thought for sure would get me sent to "the hole" where at least I'd be by myself instead of crammed in here like a rat in a sinking ship.

"We're on fucking strike, you moron," the guard announced. "I wouldn't open this cell door if I found you in there hanging."

He walked away and I stood there shivering with cold and shaking with rage. My leg was throbbing now where I'd smashed it when I'd jumped up. I hadn't eaten a thing in over 24 hours. I assessed my opponents, two big sons-o-bitches, each with at least 30 pounds on me, both of them dry from sleeping up on the bunks. I knew if I got into a cage match with these two it would be kill or be killed. I had the heart for it but I knew for sure I didn't have the strength. I spat out, "Just stay the fuck outta my face," not knowing whether that would end or ignite the confrontation. "Yo, already pissed in it," the one bastard gloated, and the other one laughed and they hi-fived each other and climbed back into their dry bunks.

I stepped over the mattress to the filthy sink and splashed both my arms and face with the trickle of cold water that came through. The scurry of mice underfoot echoed the shuffling of other men in their cells. There was a constant hum of shuffling bodies, furtive scurrying and voices, some loud, some hushed, all of them edged with danger, fear, greed. I watched as a fat cockroach picked its way over the thick grease and grime to the edge of the sink. I pushed my thumb up against the mouth of the faucet and hit the roach with a jet of cold water. It sprang from the sink and hit the floor with a clicking sound. I lost sight of it as it scurried into the shadows underneath the bunk.

By now, savvy mice had already laid claim to the mattress. I had no intention of laying down on it again, anyway. I spent the rest of the night crouched on top of the steel stool I had smashed my leg into earlier. I would have killed for a smoke, as many in this place had done already before me. Smokes, dope, pills, whatever anybody had that was more than you had was fair game. Easier to get killed in here for a pack of smokes than it was in the war in Vietnam, they tell you. Just keep your mouth shut, your eyes open and show no fear.

There are eighteen cells in this "range," with two electric doors at one end of the living area and another door outside the second set of bars, leading to outside the range. The first of the two doors inside the living area has to close behind you before they open the second door to let you in or out. The controls are located in the guard's room at one end of the range.

Along the front of the cells, between the cell bars and another wall of bars is a common area where two steel tables are planted into the concrete floor. A T.V. is stuck high up on this steel-bar wall and it's covered with Plexiglas, too. At the opposite end from the electric doors, are the common showers and a sink and two toilets, all of which are exposed to full view at all times. Privacy is an unheard of commodity.

Inside the cells, the bunks are not the originals but retain the original design of two-foot-wide steel pads clamped to concrete that hadn't been modified in almost a century. The art of functionality had reached its zenith within these walls.

Heating vents, where they exist, pump out cool air on most days, unwarmed by the heating coils that were designed to reheat fresh air from the outside. Like everything else in the inmates' quarters, the heating system is never serviced and burned out heating coils lay year after year in cold silence.

A punching bag hangs in the middle of the floor, in front of the shower area. At the other end, close to the outer doors, there are two phones, from which only outgoing calls can be placed. Prisoners fight over the phones, like they fight over everything else. You can get yourself killed over a phone call in this place.

The guards never actually step inside the living area. A corridor runs the length of the range, and a wall of steel bars separates it from the living area. The guards, if they must, walk this corridor and can see into the cells without actually going into the range.

The door outside the second set of bars is only opened when you're leaving the range, which you don't ever do, except to go to court or for visits that happen behind the ever-present Plexiglas and are ten minutes long if you're lucky. Visits are restricted to twice a week so you spend pretty much 24 hours a day, seven days a week penned inside this range with thirty–five other guys sharing space meant to house eighteen people on a temporary basis.

The smell of blood is always faintly present, sandwiched between the stench of urine and armpits and unwashed hair. Like its prisoners, the jail traps its smells forever in its walls. Trapped in the threads of the coveralls so that even when you put on clean ones the smells clamp onto your skin, seizing hold of the pores in your nostrils and embedding themselves in your memory.

Beyond the walkway, eighteen-inch thick concrete is punctured by two windows, too high to see out of but enough to remind you that there is a world outside. So, occasionally you remember there exists a world beyond "the Don," this frothy drowning river washing everything in your life up to this point into a hazy, distant memory.

On the other side of the windowless concrete wall at the back of the cells, is another eighteen-cell range just like this one, housing thirty–six other men, huddled in dark lumps or stretched out on steel bunks, one eye always open. Treachery, greed, hopelessness surrounds you, envelops you like a coffin. Left in here long enough a man could come to find comfort in the familiarity of it. It is then that compassion, human kindness, honesty become foreign, even life-threatening sensibilities. A man must learn to fight to maintain the familiar crush of fear that he wears as a cloak about his shoulders.

Back in the moment, my three-men-to-a-cell hell, the stench of piss was thick and unavoidable; even holding my breath didn't help because the next breath was deeper and then I could even taste it in the back of my throat. In the midst of it hung the lingering, pungent sweetness of the coffee that the guard had held in his hand when he came to "investigate." I stuck to shallow breaths and half closed my eyes again, allowing the "chush, chush" of the scrabbling and shuffling and rattle-voiced murmurs lull me into a half-sleep.

I daydreamed of W's bed and the fluffy duvet and the warmth of her arm draped over me. I thought about a million times of calling her but every time I thought of it, I lost my nerve. I just couldn't drag her into this mess. And one thought kept pounding at me, "I'll find a way to make it up to her. I'll find a way."

W's Chapter Two

My fingers hit the keys automatically, I don't read what I'm keyboarding as it appears on the screen but almost by sensing it, an error is corrected before my mind has fully registered and the fingers breeze along in an unbroken rhythm. I look idly across the room to the window, the City's great penis looming out there just beyond the glass, my fingers keep tapping, keeping the rhythm, never missing a stroke and an "edge" is deftly corrected to read "ledge," as if by telepathy, without a glance at the screen. The notes are in a carefully scripted long-hand, the arduous work of a construction superintendent born again as a consultant who now completes house inspections for buyers.

I've been at my new job almost two weeks and already I'm at home here and my new lawyer bosses are generous with their praise of my performance so far. I'm happy for the appreciation but still it grates on me to think I've had to crawl back into the secretarial pool just to stay afloat. But a job is a paycheque and a paycheque is what I need now more than ever before.

It's been two weeks, as well, since M. was arrested. Such an irony that my first morning back at a real job followed a long night of frantic pacing and crying alternating with desperate phone calls to almost every lawyer listed in the yellow pages with a 24-hour number. The first one to call me back was the one I hired. He seemed kind and said he would first find out where M. was and then call me right back. He called back—ten minutes where I held every breath as though it would be my last—and my hand shook so much I could barely hold the receiver. He had found him, he was in "the Don," which meant little to me until the weekend after his arrest, my first chance to visit.

"The Don" experience seemed completely surreal, out of some medieval nightmare. But I didn't wake up from it, though I prayed to, the whole time.

And now, two weeks later it was familiar to me, almost normal. A routine of sorts had begun to develop, and first thing Saturday and Sunday morning I would get up early out of bed and rush to get dressed and drive down to stand and wait outside in the cold, determined to get in for a visit. I learned from the others that you have to get there early to get in at all, now that the strike was on. I learned this only by eavesdropping, I hadn't yet had the courage to speak to anyone. Was it lack of courage or was it just a lurking hope that by staying invisible I may just wake up after all—wake to brush away the tears of a nightmare sleep?

Sleep was certainly almost a forgotten thing these days. I could manage a slumber at best. And that too had become shrouded with ritual for me, an established habit now of giving up on sleep after two hours of dozing and waking, dozing and waking, each time the wakening more startling and dis-appointing as reality reasserted itself. And then I would crawl out of bed and wrap my housecoat around me—the one that M. had bought me last Christmas; it had become his comforting arms holding me every night. I slept with it draped across the bed—a shield against the hollowness of sleeping alone. And every night for the past two weeks I had risen from my sleepless rest and draped M's surrogate arms around me.

With a cup of peppermint tea, I would curl up on the sofa and usually through tears I watched the late late movie until finally, one eye would droop and then the other and somewhere towards morning I wake to find I've sneaked a few hours sleep past my vigilant anxiety.

And so, this now is my life. What that life really is, is anyone's guess. I walk through life like it's a play and I simply play the role as it demands. It's only the owl eyes of the night that won't let me hide behind the comfort of my phoney facade. My new co-workers think I'm single, no husband, no lover, not a male in sight. I've even toyed with the idea of pretending I'm gay so nobody "suspects" anything. So bizarre, that because he is there behind every thought, I fear their imagined suspicion; and being found out would not only be facing all the shame but the absolute certainty that I'd lose this job. After all, even though it was only real estate, they *were* lawyers. How would it look for their secretary to be tied to a *criminal?!*

I shuddered at the thought and turned to look at the screen. The report was completed as though by disembodied hands, so removed was I to the content of the task. Now I waited as one at a time the printed pages emerged. I smiled as my boss passed by my desk and he nodded Good Morning to me, obviously pleased to see me at work so early. The smile is stuck to my face as I carefully mouth the words I have already rehearsed, "Oh, yes I had a wonderful weekend, thank-you for asking." I turn back to retrieve the last page as it is spat out by the printer and for a split second the smile slides off my frozen face. Horrified, I feel the warm bulge of a tear beginning to collect at the corner of my eye. I flick it away with practised secrecy and the smile is carefully arranged in place before I turn to face him. I resume my accomplished composure, the very definition of carefree, rested, poise. A perfect assistant in perfect control.

I take an invisible bow to the roaring applause of my secret audience as I graciously accept my first academy award.

Chapter Three

MARCH 18, 19___
Dear M.,

> *Hi Sweetie. It's hard to write when I'm feeling so down, but you said you wanted to have letters to read, so I'm writing.*
>
> *It was good to see you today, it always makes me feel better to be able to talk to you and especially to see that you're OK, not beat up or anything.*
>
> *It was such a relief to finally talk on the phone last night. But after you said that about "Do you think you can do this?" I really fell apart because I honestly DON'T KNOW what I can or can't do anymore.*
>
> *Last night the reality and the pain of all this just swept over me and the despair was unbearable. I cried for hours and finally fell asleep and then woke up crying again. The thought of having gone through everything we've gone through in the past six years—both together and apart—and then finally, having my life given back to me again, i.e. a great job, a beautiful home, all my needs met and no more anxiety over whether or not I can pay the rent and feed my kids—and now this.*
>
> *Anyway, now you see why I don't want to write. I want to cheer you up, but I can't be dishonest. Every word, every moment we share now is too precious, there can be no dishonesty, nothing put on or faked. You too, please don't just tell me you're fine if you're not. You know how much honesty means to me and if I can't even be honest with my best friend, then who?*

When you came back to me the last time my walls were so thick and I thought for sure you'd never get through them. I thought for sure I had put you outside of my heart forever. Maybe that's why it hurts all the more, for having taken those walls down and knowing, undeniably, unquestionably, that I hold you at the very core of my heart, the deepest part of my soul is where I love you.

Don't let my sadness right now get to you, it'll pass. During the week I'm pretty good, since work occupies my time and I can pretty much get lost in it. I really love being at work again, everything about it that I used to hate—the constant movement, so many people and deadlines and downtown traffic—I feel alive again. Unemployment is so devastating and the damage is so subtle you don't realize the depth of it until it's over. I really am grateful in spite of our circumstances, for all the good that is in my life right now. If I can only stay focussed on the good and think less about the heartache.

I phoned your lawyer as soon as I got home but it was only the machine. I left a message asking about canteen money and the pre-trial and also asked him to call you if he knows anything more about a court date for the guilty plea.

Talk to you soon (I hope)!

Love, W.

April 2, 19__

Dear W.,

So! Here it is six weeks later and finally the first letter. My writing utensils are pretty inadequate, the pencil is about one and a half inches long, I have no hard surface to write on (except the filthy floor, in which case the paper would get all stinked up), one piece of torn paper and too much to say. But reading and smelling your letters have really inspired me today.

Today is the first day after the strike has finally ended and perhaps it won't take long to get this letter out to you. The living conditions in this hole don't seem much improved, but at least we aren't locked up 24 hours a day. After dinner (if you want to call unidentifiable boiled mush, "food"—where the HELL do the newspapers get those stories of prisoners eating steak, anyway?), the phones are open until 8:30 p.m., so hopefully we can get to chat once or twice through the week. Sorry it has to be collect, I hope you can handle the phone bills.

You're wondering why I don't write to you and honestly you would have to be here to really understand, but suffice it to say the noise level in here is always so loud, constant movement, constant clattering and clanging and voices and ...oh, god, Sweetie, just sitting down to say the simplest things is so difficult. But I'll try to be more conscientious about writing to you and always know that even if I haven't written, not a day goes by—hell, not an hour goes by, that I don't think of you.

You keep asking for reassurance that things will be different when this is all over. You know I'm not as good with words as you are, but I am going to try to sum it all up for you.

When you get put in a place like this and everything in your material existence is taken away, including the people you love, the only safe place you have to turn is inward. If you spend enough time there, you develop knowings. I don't mean searching your soul for answers. I mean just sitting in silence, not trying to concentrate or distract yourself with any specific method of breathing or searching out the answer to any one question. Just sitting still and alert and being receptive to your body's little messages telling you where you need to relax, what muscles or joints need to let go a bit. Being open to whatever impulses your mind and soul send to you, you are able to teach yourself, I mean, some place of greater wisdom inside you is able to release something, and new truths are revealed.

I have learned some new truths in this way. All of these truths are governed by the strongest power source in the universe. Love. A great, deep, all-encompassing pool of Love that we are free to drink from, dive into, bask in, as often as we wish, as often as we allow ourselves to do so.

Once you become capable of sending and receiving Love at all times in spite of your circumstances or the emotions of the moment, you pretty much become the Master of Life. I sure don't think that you or I are at that level yet, but the important thing is that I recognize that this is the goal. And this I promise you: When this episode of our lives is over, I will love you more than any other human being ever has or ever will be able to love. Not just because I should or because of all the support and help you have been to me in here. But because I need to love you. It nourishes my soul to love you. Not just anybody, you. Because YOU are the ONLY one.

You carry the lessons I need to learn in THIS life, and I carry yours and in this life together, we shall create miracles. For me, just having you in my life is a miracle.

Thank-you again for not losing faith.

Love, M.

April 6, 19__

Dear M,

Thank-you for your letter (finally). I hear what you're saying about how hard it is to write while you're in there, but even the sight of your handwriting, knowing you had touched the paper and held the envelope in your hands... it made me cry, and I slept with your envelope and letter under my pillow last night. Laugh if you want to, I know how sappy it is. But this separation, not even being able to touch, I never knew how much a touch could mean. How do people survive losing a lover to death? I can't even imagine how it would feel to never touch you again.

I just don't know two people who were more meant to be together than you and I. And all the good you've always wanted to do for every-one, it will all still happen, sweetheart, don't worry, have faith.

One thing this separation is good for is that we (you) are forced to COMMUNICATE, just like I've always wanted. There's so much that can't be said, I know, and just knowing that every word of our letters gets read by some stranger keeps me from writing more of what I want to say, but still we are communicating and this is a good thing.

Maybe the next couple of years is going allow us to build our home, our relationship on the foundation we've already laid, the house of real understanding, love and commitment. And our kids will inherit the benefit of it and our grandkids, and who knows, maybe the hundredth monkey will all come out of this. Why not think big? But small too, we should think small and be happy, thrilled with all the smallest delights that life can give us, like a sunny afternoon with nothing to do but just be together, or having coffee together in the morning, or pulling out the sofa and curling up for a movie, all those wonderful tiny little things that we should value because added up together they are EVERYTHING. Everything we need, everything we want will be ours, because we have each other. We're only separated in body, it's our minds that have the real power. Even if we couldn't write, we would find a way somehow.

Do you get any reading material at all? I hope you get your canteen money, it's a dirty thing they did if they took it. The guard last time was actually nice and even decent with me, what a surprise.

Love you, W.

*A*PRIL *14, 19__*
Dear W.,

It was great to see you. I'm sorry you had to wait so long to get in. I know it must be pretty disgusting in that visit room, but amplify that by about 10,000 times on this side of the glass. I honestly never knew such people really existed. Well, I guess I knew but you know how it is, you don't think about these things until you're forced to—and you're right, this time has been given to me as a gift to force me to think about and face all the things I've been running away from all these years.

I'm feeling pretty good about this new lawyer. In spite of his pretty bleak forecast I think the bottom line will turn out OK. In any case, I feel a lot safer going into court with a guilty plea and a lawyer who has some respect in the courtroom. I wish we hadn't wasted so much time on Mr. S., incompetent as he was, but that's legal aid for you. It's not the innocent that go free, it's them that can afford the best lawyers. O.J. is a case in point.

Guaranteed, if I hadn't been so down on my luck in the first place to get myself into this predicament, if I had been a greedy son-of-a-bitch wanting to just get more money for the sake of having more, I would be able to pay some big-ass Bay Street lawyer to get me off scot-free.

In my case, I did the crime and so I can live with the punishment. But in so many cases in here, these guys really are helpless victims of circumstance, poverty, ignorance and hopelessness. They don't even stand a chance of ever recovering from their totally fucked-up lives. They are in here not just because they've committed crimes (mostly drug-related and mostly they, themselves, are the only real victims) but because they are poor.

But there's another side of the whole system that I just can't figure out for the life of me. For instance, take the man who gets ten years in prison for robbing a bank. No previous record, no one hurt in the robbery, the man is unemployed, desperate, he does something stupid, out of control.

Then take a look at the man who rapes an eighty-year-old woman at gunpoint, or another who commits numerous sexual attacks on children, or another who attempts to murder five of his own family members leaving them for dead while he goes out to a bar for a few pints. The lasts three are actual examples of men who have been treated as "sick people," which undoubtedly they are, but they are "treated" for a total of maybe two to three years. Then (if they survive the beatings, etc., from other inmates), they are let back out on the street again, not because their sickness is cured, but because they are INCURABLE. Which means they will want to go out and do it again, they can't stop themselves.

Meanwhile, the bank robber only wanted money. He didn't feel that he was stealing from any person, but from an institution (one that we know robs us all, but does it legally.)

Now, looking at the punishments given out to the two different types of criminals, what does it tell you about the society we live in? If you are desperate for money and you rob a bank you are punished for ten years, but if your "sickness" causes you to go out and rape and murder inno-cent people, then we'll try to fix you up (though we won't try too hard) and if we can't fix you, we'll let you go. Go figure?! The only real justice for rapists happens inside, taken into the hands of the prisoners. Of course, PC (Protective Custody) can prevent that some of the time, but I've heard—and seen—some pretty unbelievable stuff. Vigilante justice at its most extreme.

Anyway, sitting on this side of the fence (the bars) really shows you some ugly truths about our society and raises some very confusing ques-tions. But of course, I haven't forgotten the value of a buck. Money sure does make your life a lot easier. In a perfect world everyone has a job that best suits them and life is grand. This won't be the case for me when I get out and I realize that you have justifiable concerns on that issue. I used to get frustrated with nowhere or dead-end jobs or even some good ones I had where I lost interest. I used to view life as being so short and I had to get everything done all at once. Of course that's impossible, so I would get frustrated and depressed and end up doing nothing. This of course amplified the original problem and then I would get angry and blame everyone around me or expect them to dive in and save me or drown with me.

The truth is, yes, it is important to be happy in your job but it doesn't come overnight. The trick is, if you have to work in a job that does not fulfil or uplift you then find something that does. A hobby, program or project, or write a book or something. So at the end of the week you feel some sense of accomplishment and pride and that's real wealth. The point is that bogus jobs don't have to last forever. They do, on the other hand, provide the basics of life and some peace of mind that you at least have an income, even if it's limited.

I think I have learned, from this experience, that I need to appre-ciate the "bridges" that come my way and believe in whatever I do. That great job I always wanted will come my way when I slow down and am ready to assume the responsibility it will demand of me. And no matter what job I do in the meantime, I have to be GOOD at it, the best I can be; that is very important for one's state of mind because it feels so bad to lose a nowhere job just because of lack of interest, when you know deep down inside that given half a chance (yourself giving you half a chance), you could have done that job and your boss's job, too.

Sweetie, I know now how to make my chances happen. You will never have to worry about me pulling my weight or making irresponsible financial decisions again. I have such a clear view of the whole picture, now. Not just where I want us to be in ten years but how to get us there. I am certainly not happy or grateful to be in this place, but what a school it can be. On a spiritual level, you can learn here in one year, what it would take probably 50 years to learn on the outside. Flip side, of course, if you don't choose to take the lessons and understand your problems, you could go straight downhill.

Thank-you again, for not losing faith.

Love you forever, M.

Chapter Four

I was so glad to be in from the cold I simply stood at the top of the staircase, shoulders hunched but not shivering, letting the warmth sink in where it could, through my chilled bones. I didn't stamp my feet or unfold my arms, just stood quietly breathing as if, to make a sound, I'd be thrown back out to brave the icy whips hammering on the outside door.

I thought of those who were on the street tonight, I hadn't lifted a finger to help any of "the people" today, or yesterday, in fact I couldn't recall the last time I'd helped any street person, no roof over their heads, avoided by most eyes, panhandling in the passageways of the underground maze where we spent our winter shopping hours.

Why hadn't I thought of them lately? Why was I buying my children frozen pizza and burritos for after-school when other children didn't have a can of soup on the shelves? How had I put them out of my mind so easily, so quickly, now that I wasn't one of them anymore? But that was it, and the thought was a relief and I stopped hugging myself so hard and began to unbutton my down-filled coat. A coat I wouldn't have dreamed of buying myself two years before.

I had put them out of my mind in fear. I wanted to forget, deliberately forget the despair, the hopelessness of poverty. I wasn't one of them anymore, why would I want to allow them any mind-space? My mind was full of more invigorating things now, paying off my car, buying new boots for the boys, making my home all cosy and full of beautiful things again, and getting ahead, yes, kissing ass and getting ahead.

I recall my days in other battlefields, warring with the smug and heartless whores at the Welfare office. I had limped home then, in dented armour, kicked and beaten by their idiotic questions and robotic probing, how stupid they looked behind their glass barriers keeping the enemy out. I had become public enemy Number One—the single mother. How easy it was to think instead of buying food I could just buy two bottles of pills and be out of it once and for all. And five pills later the lunacy slips away and laid bare beneath it is the real desire to survive, to say *I didn't quit, I didn't fail this time,* be there and see how it all turns out in the end. I just want to be there. God, I just want to *stay* ... and be there.

I finally, slowly uncurl my arms and take my coat off, still hugging it close to me, convincing myself that this wonderful, warm coat is mine, this beautiful apartment is mine, no one will take this from me ever again.

I'm safe. I'm really, truly safe. I sit down on the top step and bury my face in my coat and cry.

APRIL 20, 19__
Dear M.,

Didn't get to talk to you again today, but thanks for the message you sent. Were you just worried that I'd be waiting and upset? I've gotten used to you not being able to call. I take it in stride now, even though it is disappointing.

I have to say, I'm a little worried about us living together after all this is over. We've tried it so many times, followed our hearts and tried to live together and you know what happened every single time.

There's lots of questions, like are you going to be able to carry your half of the expenses, maybe not immediately but pretty soon after you get out? Will you stick to whatever it is you decide on? So far in one month I've heard you mention about three different ideas for getting work, all of them good ideas and I know you're just thinking out loud and this is very good, but you do have to settle on something eventually and plan it out so that when you do get out it'll run smoothly with no down time and no discouraging setbacks. You are so bright and so capable of doing very well in a legitimate business, making a legitimate living. You just have to make up your mind that doing it slowly is OKAY. I know that anything you set your mind to, you will accomplish but somehow you have to discipline yourself, tame your impatience and understand that doing it slowly is not so bad.

In the past I haven't or we have not been able to reasonably discuss things or I just let things happen and ended up resenting a lot of it. And the truth is I feel like I did try so hard in the first few years to make everything work and to be a family. I don't think that back then you appreciated how much I had to give up and how hard I worked at trying to look after your kids and how much added responsibility that was when my kids were already so grown up. And the truth is that now I don't want to go there again.

Think about all of this and please give me a response after you've had time to think it all over, and without getting all defensive.

I know you miss your kids terribly. If you want (if you don't get bail) I can get a birthday card for C. and mail it to you so you can write in it and send it to her. Tell me right away 'cause there's only three weeks to get it to you and then to her. Do you want me to do something for them for Easter? Would their mother let me?

I would really like to try to maintain some kind of relationship with them while you're in there. I don't want to be a stranger in their lives when we get back together.

Well, I guess this letter got long enough. You write back to me about all of this and I'll keep an open mind too, I promise.

Love, W.

April 29, 19__

Hi Sweetie-pie,

I promised you a letter before the weekend so here it is. Well, we are going into the third month now and even though I was hoping to be sentenced by now, I have already served six months dead time, seven if you count the strike time. It's not a sure thing that they'll count the time in here waiting as double-time or even count it at all, but let's take as positive a view as possible.

So, I told you I would respond to your letter about the issue of us living together when this is all over, and I'm glad I decided to write about it rather than speak to you, because it gave me a chance to think first. This way, I can consider all the pros and cons, the whys and why nots, without barking out a defensive response (which has been the norm for me) and then it won't be so difficult to make a responsible decision that will satisfy everyone's needs.

First, I think I should point out that in spite of how much you tried to dull the edges, I realize you've had a lot of time to think about it and are somewhat panicked at the thought of us living together again. So "a little bit concerned" is very subtle of you and I thank you for trying to spare my feelings but I just want you to know that I know just how worried you really are.

I'm not upset at all that you are worried about it. Of course you're worried, you damn well should be given our track record. Look at all the places we have lived in the past five years. Looking back and think-ing hard I can honestly say that in every place you always tried as hard as you could to make everyone comfortable. You even sacrificed the needs of your own children in many cases to satisfy my seemingly impossible desire to make my kids feel a sense of home with me. I not only always took it for granted, it became an expectation. Like so many other things. So Sweetie, from the bottom of my heart, before we can move forward, I need you to accept my apology.

I have just taken about forty minutes to think and I really don't think it's fair for me to expand on my ideas on this issue until I have heard your response to what I've just said. I have a lot of good ideas about how we can make things work, practically speaking, but I don't want to take anything else for granted and I want us to take our time on this and move at the same pace.

So let's agree to make this a process. I think it will give us both the space we need to think deeply about every little detail and not make hasty decisions out of fear or guilt or even love. The truth is, I'm happy that you feel "a little concerned," which really means you're downright terrified of it, but that just tells me that you want it to work as much as I do. Please don't ever forget how much I love you.

Love, M.

MAY 12, 19__
Dear M.,

It's the night before the bail hearing and I'm feeling panicky. Your lawyer finally called me to go over briefly the kind of questions I'll be asked.

Hearing the reality of what I'm doing really shocked me. If you were to take off they would come after me for whatever money I put up as a bond—$10-15,000—and then I really would be up shit's creek. And for the first time since this whole thing happened I really have felt some terrible doubts creep in—like what if it IS just a con game you're playing, what if you ARE just trying to get out of jail so you can take off, or what if you're totally sincere but once you get out you get some crazy notion (and GOD KNOWS you've had some doozies, and NO ONE can talk you out of anything once you get your mind made up) that you could take off and never come back, etc. etc. All these terrible doubts and the only thing I can do is go over again in my mind all that we've said between us, both before and after. I remember the night you took me out for dinner, when I was still going out with R. and you asked me to marry you. I know you meant every word you said that night. I know how much you really loved me and it's true that even while I was seeing someone else you hung around to just be my friend and you didn't go out with anyone else.

I read your old letters again, hoping to find some comfort and some strength there. One of them is a mad letter, you wrote it when we split up the first time and you left all your stuff behind. I kept that letter because I wanted to remember what you were like when you were mad at me. Funny but reading it now, all I see is hurt. All I see is how much you wanted to come back to me then and didn't know how.

But the other letter is the one that always makes me cry. You wrote it after we met again, in the park, after your broken neck. (Why is it you always wait til you get broken before you come back to me?) You wrote to tell me that you couldn't be just my friend, this was after I had met R. And at the end of the letter you say—just to have it said—that you would give anything for a second chance. And I don't remember how we *eventually got back together that time, I think you changed your mind about not being my friend and things went from there. God only knows for sure what was in your mind all those times you left me, why you kept on leaving even after knowing that leaving me was impossible.*

And now we get back to the questions I'll be asked tomorrow. The most difficult one being, "What makes you think you can control him?" (Your lawyer used the word control, meaning, control your behaviour so that you'll show up for trial.) And I guess the answer is, 1) because he wants to get on with his life and 2) because he's never lied to me before (which is true, although you have broken many promises) and 3) because he is utterly devoted to me. And I know if I really believe it, reason number three will be most powerful because it feels powerful to say it and think it. He is utterly devoted to me. He would never leave if it means being separated from me. He would never do that to me, have me risk what little I have and then run out on me. I must believe in you, and without being able to hear your voice and see your eyes, it's so hard to dispel the doubts. You won't know it tomorrow, you won't know it until you read this letter next week, but tomorrow when I tell them that I know beyond a shadow of a doubt that you will not put me in the position of hardship that it would place on me if you were to run out, I will have spent the night convincing myself that it's true.

Last night the strangest thing happened, and now that I remember it I don't feel as scared. About 10:00–10:30 p.m. I had the unmistakable feeling that you were with me. I was lying in bed reading and I FELT you, it was so strong and so incredibly sweet. It didn't make me cry or anything, I just felt safe and loved and wanted. And I even woke up feeling the same way, that I had just been with you and you had held me and comforted me and I felt your strength.

I'm going to go to bed and try to feel that same feeling I had last night, the feeling of your arms around me, holding me, keeping me safe and loved.

M., I love you so much. I hope that we'll be together again soon.

Love, W.

May 23, 19__
Dear W,

Hi Sweetie! Miss the hell out of ya. I've been having some pretty neat meditations lately and I had to write and tell you about the one I had last night.

I was just sitting still having cleared my mind and body of stress and tension. Then, these images just started shooting into my head. They were coming in the form of white light surrounded by darkness (like words on a chalkboard). Some were almost like voices. The neat thing is that I recognized right away that these images were not coming from my own mind or thoughts because of the way the sentences were structured. "You" and "your" and stuff like that. I became instantly aware that I was receiving instructions from some other source—Sweetie, I have to tell you that I couldn't repeat this to another soul 'cause I know you're the only person I could tell this to who wouldn't say I had gone off the deep-end into some kind of schizophrenic episode or some such bullshit.

Anyway, back to the "instructions." They started very simply and got more elaborate as I consciously strengthened the connection. I was even able to stop for a moment to write things down and then "go back in." I did this a few times.

Here are a few of them. I'm not sure what they all mean yet:

"Get Clear."
"You are looking for something."
"Express yourself."
"You have ability."
"You don't have to be perfect."
"Stand up for who you are."
"Your kids need you."
"There is a problem with your mother's death."
"You must take better care of your health."
"The flow of energy is restricted in your body due to toxins (smoking)."
The last two I found really informative:

"Your fear of confrontations and the necessity to avoid them in this place have you confused."

Earlier in the week I had done a lot of work around fear of confrontation because it had been a problem for years, as you know. So the message for me was clear. Even though I am ready and able to overcome this fear now, this is not the time or the place to do so. A mistake could mean a life or death situation.

Last one. It's a doozie:

> *"You had to go to jail in order to learn faster. You and W. would not have made it if you hadn't come here. This was a necessary event in the evolution of your relationship."*

That one almost put me into tears. I went to sleep that night grateful to be in jail. I woke up knowing that I had to take a closer look at my mother's death.

Love you, M.

Chapter Five

I sit down to write and sip my coffee a few times thinking back on all the billions of words that have travelled through my head today, none of them arranged in any pattern I can use. I feel the brain fatigue, brain-fog, my inside head covered by a sly and lacy gauze of complacency that smothers the breath of inspiration even before it has struggled to be taken in.

Still, sometimes that breath succeeds and a word or phrase is born. The reds and golds and indigos of dreams drift in and settle themselves into worthy notes, arranged on the page in fairly satisfying tones and rifts and melodies. And the mystery of the Muse remains unsolved, content as I am to simply have Her visit and stay as long as She will, at least until She tires of my lethargy and fed-up with having to constantly tug at my boot-straps, the Lady leaves in a huff.

Indignantly, I protest, *but I was trying, I simply needed a break, a coffee, some bathroom relief...* okay, enough of this She says, relenting. Lady Muse returns again to the spinning wheel.

Today is Monday. I had promised myself that on Mondays I would write. No matter what, I would set aside Mondays to write.

It's so cold outside and I've just come home from a hard day at the office. Oh, a bath would be heaven... NO, the Lady stamps her foot, she warns me one last time. I must write.

I came home planning to make dinner for all of us to have together for a change—so many comings and goings now with their teenage social calendars booked so solid I can barely get a family dinner in edgewise... so much food in the fridge, I open it and leave the door standing open and then swing all the cupboard doors open and finally yank open the freezer door too and I spin around slowly in a "360" surveying my stock full o' chock full o' safety, full of food, we wouldn't go hungry this winter. Not ever again. And not a box of Kraft Dinner in sight.

Content at just seeing the food and all the possibilities it offers, I decide not to make dinner after all. We'll order pizza—just because we can.

No dinner to make, no dishes and laundry demanding my attention, no groceries to be bought, no shelves to repair, no plants to save the life of with last yellow leaves withering off dried stumps of branches, I have time to sit down and write now, no excuses.

Who's afraid of Virginia Woolf, Virginia Woolf, Virginia Woolf? I am. I am I am I am. I could light candles and incense and attempt to invoke her spirit but God knows, I have enough trouble stemming the tide of my own madness, without risking bringing hers flooding in on me too. Madness they call it. I wonder if a man wrote that little biography in the front of her book, god wouldn't she just be rolling over in her grave now or no, she'd laugh at the irony of it, the humour wouldn't be lost even on herself.

Was she mad? Genius, surely. But madness, is it a flip of the coin? She took her own life at fifty–nine. God, that's only twenty years away for me. I've already made one attempt. Will that be written of me ... *plagued by recurrent bouts of madness and poverty, she never did find the time to sit down and write.* Madness and poverty revolving, and overlapping sometimes just long enough that the two of them conceived the demon-child *Desperation.*

But anyway, here I am then, not plagued by madness or hunger but what is it now? Fatigue? Brain fatigue? What, surely you can't be fatigued after *a day at the office* holding up pathetic and flailing egos with one hand, typing furiously with the other? Eyes and ears attuned to every pearl of wisdom spoken by those rugged men full of intelligent ideas spouted so eloquently atop barstools at the "Choo Choo" lounge.

Fatigued by what? By forcing my mouth and throat to make that cooing sound of awe and wonder at their clearly superior knowledge and abilities while voices inside me scream, "Help! They're murdering me!" That tiny wisp of soul identity a voice still audible beneath the avalanche of obedience, I must be good, I must be good, I must not lose this job, and I betray my soul with every nod of agreement across flawless mahogany finishes.

I watch my own two sons struggling with their identities and I know that because of me they are here and somehow I have to help them bore a path through this unforgiving stone of life. I pray they won't become one of them, won't go home to disappointed wives who tire of shovelling endless heaps of coal into ego furnaces, please god let them be happier than that. The Lady gently reminds me that the keyboard awaits.

Too fatigued to write.

What is this GREAT WORK that will not let me rest, will not leave me in peaceful, self-absorbed, blissful, unconscious, uncaring ignorance? Goddam, will it ever let me go? Have I been bitten by some supernatural spider, a mother spider fighting to bring her children into awareness of the web and their responsibility in it, for it, to weave it, love it, protect it, and not ever forget it?

And so, yes Virginia, it is you and I alone tonight and yes, by god, I AM afraid of you. My god, you write like a ... and these three dots represent three individual seconds of being at a loss for words. Metaphor, that's where you shine—like the lights you write about, red and gold and indigo...

The web.

I lay silent, watchful of the night.

Thoughts ran like currents through my weary and unwilling brain, my will pitted against the incessant urging of words that pressed themselves deeply into the flesh of my mind, hot and insistent. There was nothing for it but to get up out of bed and return to the keyboard.

All day I had sat like an expectant bride, fingers poised, the odd word leaping up and out and planting itself on the screen, saucy and mocking in its utter detachment from structure or sentence or paragraph. An incomplete thought scurrying about seeking playmates, and finally, finding none, it would slump, dejected, to the bottom of the screen, indifferent to my pleas to go forth and multiply. An unpregnant pause ensued. I finally crawled to bed, daunted and despairing of whether I would ever understand the capricious habits of the Muse.

And now, with me beaten and groggy with anticipated sleep, She is ready to play and play along I must. I return to the scene of my humiliation and the fingers pound the keys with abandoned deliberation, strike-strike-strike, not a breath or pause between letters that spread into words that flow like sap in the Springtime.

It's the wee hours of morning before I can crawl back to bed and I can barely recall a single word that has sprung from my fingertips.

June 5, 19__
Dear M.,

Just got your amazing letter! Awesome, Sweetie. I'm so proud of you for FINALLY tuning in. I always knew you could, if only you would stand still long enough to give it a chance. It really gives me hope, Sweetie, that we really will get through all this in one piece.

I finally wrote a bit today, not much, but more than I've written since all this happened. It's a shame too, 'cause I was really on a roll that weekend you got arrested, before I knew about it of course. Anyway, of course it's been too hard to write anything, there's too much that I'm feeling and it's too hard to put my thoughts together sensibly.

This is pretty rough and probably needs a lot of cleaning up but it puts a few of my thoughts into words. I mean, there's so much to be said about this whole situation that I couldn't possibly say it all in one piece. There's so many angles, so many themes. There's all the anger that I have over your choice to go this way, to do what you did, even if I understand how you came by that way of thinking. Still, understanding it doesn't make me less angry about it.

But that theme doesn't belong in this piece. I wrote this today when I ran across a little newspaper article about a woman losing her husband—actually I'll send it to you, J. got this tiny little "newspaper" (a promotional thing) and he saved it for you 'cause he thought it would fit nicely into an envelope and you'd be happy to have a "newspaper" (he really is a very sweet kid).

Anyway, I read this article that's in it and I could relate so much to her grief except for the fact that she can talk about it, tell everyone about it, ask for their comfort and support and not feel ashamed or embarrassed or fearful of being discovered.

And the only reason I am all those things is because I don't want to be made to suffer from the cruelty and judgements of others. I don't want the kids to be subjected to their judgements and ridicule, although I still question why I give a damn, why it matters to me at all what people say. But somehow it still grates on me when I think that they would have the opportunity to judge me, to somehow count me as less than them for the fact that I have allowed myself to become part of this by being loyal to you.

I guess I'm angry at myself too, for even caring what anybody thinks. I wish I didn't give a damn. I really truly hope I get to where I just don't care. Where I know so profoundly that in being true to loving you, to understanding your actions and forgiving your egotism in bar-relling through with this crazy scheme, to never forgetting the truth of our connection and how much we love each other, my spirit is true and good and I am acting on the very highest of ideals—serving love and justice and truth, and what higher ideals can there ever be than those.

So here's the little piece I just wrote:

I've been reading about grieving—not intentionally, I haven't sought out any of the dozens of books written on the subject, available in the "self-help" or "psychology" section of the bookstore. I've made a point of avoiding those books, fearing I'll find in their pages too close a mirror, too close a recording of the thoughts in my own head, the feelings in my heart written down and displayed for all to see, to read, to perhaps relate to but never, never to understand.

Grief is the loneliest emotion. It doesn't matter how many people have experienced it before you, under circumstances seemingly identical (it's never really identical, nobody has the same relationship with the loved one that you had), but being unique, the relationship requires it's own grief experience. The isolation perhaps is lessened when there are others around you to lend kind words, to offer condolences, to at least listen to your pain. But grieving is a solitary journey.

Without looking for it, however, I stumble across snatches of other people's thoughts, voices of grief. And sometimes I catch myself in time and close off my own feelings, quickly shut the lid down hard on my heart, forcing down the springs of tears that only wait for the merest opportunity to well up and burst my well-disciplined heart and head and eyes into weeping and sobs. Sometimes I just have to ride it out until it's over.

The hardest part of this has been the utter aloneness. I can tell no one of my pain. I carry on through all the motions of life as though all is well and normal in my home and my heart. My family calls from far away and I force a cheery note into my voice, yes everything's fine, oh yes, we're all well, yes the kids are fine, everything's great, yes, Happy Easter to you too... (Click. Breathe. Sigh. A tear. Wipe it away. They'd never understand. It's okay. I'm okay. I'll get myself through this.)

He didn't die. If he had died I could tell everyone, I could wail and cry and vent all my anger. Everyone would bear witness to my pain and desolation and the fear of being alone at night with no one to hold me after a bad dream. And there would be no shame, no excuses to be made, no raised eyebrows or heads shaking or clucking or tsking or worse, the things-they-would-do to thinly veil their scathing judgements behind hollow gestures of pity. *Well you made your bed... told you so... but WHY don't you just leave him... get on with your life* is all there would be to listen to, at best.

He is my best friend. How is it that everyone talks about loyalty as if they've been there but none of them have ever known the treasure that we hold between us?

Yes he's hurt me. Many times. And this one isn't even the worst of it. Yes he has seemingly deserted me at times, but I know what was in his heart. I know they all call me a fool but they simply do not know, cannot possibly know what I know of him. They have never been there, right inside his heart, where I have been, where I have lived for six years.

And so to avoid their reproaches, the desolation of being forever and hopelessly misunderstood, my grief remains silent. And it troubles me less now, it seems to have found comfort in laying quietly in wait until a crack in my armour lets it seep out and run me ragged for a few hours.

Why did he do it? Why wouldn't he? How many of them would do the same if they thought they could get away with it? How many of them have wished, dreamed of defying law and order and government and the crushing power of conformity, hopelessness, the injustice of wealth and misused power that eventually squeezes our souls into dried up prunes until not even a phantom memory of freedom remains?

How many of them keep themselves from doing what they really want to do and content themselves with becoming barstool-soap box revolutionaries, wasting their anger amongst ignorant ears, accomplishing nothing? And yet it is just those ones who will be quickest to judge, first to turn their backs if I were to say to them, "He couldn't take being on the bottom anymore. He robbed a bank. Now he's in prison. And I'm alone." Would they be there to hush my weeping in the night?

And the forever heroes on the silver screen, bloody shoot-outs, *yeah* they all cry when the cops get blown away and the fearless hero, in his perfectly faded Levis showing his great ass to its best advantage, turns and runs to freedom, sawed off shotgun slung recklessly over his shoulder. They all cheer. They want to be like him. They want to be him. If only they had the guts.

And then it's real and they witness a "take-down" right in front of them, right in their own neighbourhood and it's suddenly *yeah for the good guys, yeah for law and order, the banks are good to us, politicians are fair and reasonable and have only the most altruistic motives...* How is it they can be so shallow, so short-sighted, so morally hollow and lacking all understanding of honour and justice?

How did honour and justice get so fucked up? How is it that an honourable man falls into such despair that he sees only motive and becomes blind to method, becoming victim to the very "justice" he expected to restore?

And these are all the thoughts I have and can't share with anyone. No, if I could say, *he's dead you know, after working for the government all these years* (as though "living" and "working for the government" weren't already a contradiction in terms), and they would sympathize and offer comfort to me in my grief, for they would understand that I had lost a "good" man and that I would be deprived of his laughter, his arms, his voice.

But he's not dead. I'm grieving over a prisoner of law and order and the un-justice system. So I grieve alone.

JUNE 6, 19__

Dear M.,

I had an amazing conversation with A. last night and it shifted my whole perspective on this awful experience.

I see all of this now as the necessary experience of having to watch my anger come up so large and unmistakable—'cause ever since this happened I've been angry at the whole world and I hate everybody and it wears me down to be so angry all the time. But the anger is undoubtedly a defence mechanism that has kicked in to protect me because I feel so fragile and close to tears at every moment. My anger balances that emotionality. So I need the anger.

But on the other hand, having it come up so undeniably and having to reckon with it gives me an opportunity to see it for what it is. It's been there, lying dormant all my life and now it's showing up. Which means that it can be healed, because I can see it and recognize it, examine it and heal the root causes as they appear to me. And more than that, it underlines that the path to healing for me now lies in being able to forgive.

I know this is the key to my next hurdle, the key to moving onward and upward. So now I'm reading this little book I bought two years ago, On Forgiveness, and I'm hoping it will help me get to the stage of WANTING to forgive, 'cause I'm not really even there yet. My only motivation is that I can't stand being this angry and lonely all the time. I can't stand hating people and keeping myself alone for the simple fact of not wanting to be around people anymore. I think this will be a big step towards my evolution.

A. is incredibly wise and insightful. He is so mature. I can't believe he's my own son. He admitted he got stuck on dope for awhile and that was one of the reasons he wanted to change schools, 'cause he realized how addictive it had become for him and he really wanted to get away from those kids who were so into it. I must have done something right in raising him, cause he came to all of this all on his own and made his own decision to clean up his act.

I'm so proud of him. And I am absolutely flabbergasted at how he has absorbed so much of what I've taught him about life and truth and

*spirituality. He really GETS IT. It is so amazing to think that this is
my SON. And so much of his wisdom and understanding comes from
listening to and watching me live my life. Yes, I live it the hard way, but
I have always been true to my self, loyal to my beliefs, willing to risk
everything in order to say and do what I believe to be true. I guess I'm
feeling pretty proud of myself right about now, too.*

*I talked to your lawyer and he mentioned money again and I told
him that he needn't worry because we are working on selling what we
can and it may take awhile, but we'll get some money to him eventually.
I didn't ask again about legal aid, I thought I should get off the subject
and leave it between you and him. Anyway, let me know what you want
me to tell him, if anything.*

Okay, so I'm gonna go now.

Love you, W.

Chapter Six

From W's Journal
JUNE 10, 19__

Alienation. Disrespect. Being less of a person. Being made less than or at least, the feeling of being less than is triggered, stirred up. And then the rage is triggered. Rage at injustice. At powerlessness.

That's what I said to him, the fat bastard, "So what is this, is this going to become a little power game here?" First he examined my I.D. as though it was suspicious, then the questions start, as though I've committed a crime, as though I don't have every right to be here and exercise my legitimate rights to visit a prisoner. And then he makes me wait an extra hour, and then maybe he'll budge his fat ass to reach over to the phone and call down to let them know there is a visitor for him and maybe if we're lucky, we'll have a visit. If he feels like it. If he gets enough satisfaction out of playing the game first.

His puffy-chested voice booms out from behind the glass, "No, there's no power struggle, here. I don't know what you're talking about," and his eyes won't meet mine and we both know he's playing the game.

He, of course, is always the big, strong cat, pampered and powerful; we, on the other side of the glass are all the little rats, his pawns, his amusement.

"Of course not," I puffy-chest him back, "there's no power struggle is there, because you're the one with all the power, aren't you?"

He sits high up on a stool behind the counter, the set-up designed to intimidate. He leans forward and his fat, red nose is almost touching the glass. His breath makes little white discs of moist air that I have to lift my eyes to watch as they disappear and reappear. "Yes, ma'am," he booms back, smugly ignorant, pleased with himself, not even recognizing what a pompous fool he has shown himself to be, not caring anyway, after all, I'm just one of "You people."

"You people." He had the gall to address me like that! "You people." I challenged him. "You people?! And just what would that 'we people' be, Sir?" And then he couldn't back down. He had gone too far and he'd have to see it through, but *he* knew that I knew he was a miserable, ignorant, powerless little cog in the wheel and all he really could do was to go round with it.

A "You people" I may well be but at least I wasn't like him, chained to a goddamn wheel of hopeless, helpless ignorance, doomed to keep on turning round and round and making believe he's the one doing the turning but knowing he's less than the man he was yesterday, just for still being there.

How to deal with this stuff? How do you just ignore it, ignore them? What do you do with the rage against injustice, disrespect? And then the feelings that follow hard on the rage—wanting just to strike out, smash them, smash *anything,* hate everything and everyone, the RAGE!! of them treating you like you are "less than."

Less what? Less worthwhile? Less deserving? Less valuable, less of a human being, having less right to be here, to breathe the same air as they do?

Just less than.

And powerless.

And all because of circumstance, simply by virtue of the fact that he applied for a job to sit on that side of the window. If the tables were turned and I were the one with the power, I would be gracious, knowing full well it was only the merest circumstance that made it so, that tomorrow or another reality would reverse our roles. And being in power, one does not need to assert anything. The power is already given. Is it not the easiest thing to do, to be gracious, when you know you have the power? What makes them so needy that the power itself is not enough for them?

I'm so tempted to imagine him stripped of his thick skin and hung out in the sun to dry like an eel. I have to make an effort to suppress my vivid imaginings, knowing how dangerous thoughts can be, how quickly and easily thought manifests itself. I suppress it only to save myself the karma that must ensue. But if karma didn't exist... if I could rage unchecked... but it does exist and as certain as I am of reaping it myself, so will he and all the ignorant blow-holes like him.

JUNE 16, 19__

M.,

So I waited two days to be able to talk to you and get this off my chest and now I'm angrier and more frustrated than ever. Two minutes with so much to talk about is just impossible. My frustration level right now is so high I really feel as though I'm going to lose it.

I am so goddamn sick and tired of being treated like I'm the criminal, like I deserve to be treated like shit just because I come to see you. I'm sick to death of feeling like a second-class citizen.

I CAN'T FUCKING TAKE ANY FUCKING MORE. I CAN'T FUCKING BE ALONE ALL THE TIME. And I feel too ashamed, too embarrassed, too much of a liar to want to be with anyone, to want any friends to know what my life is really about and how really crazed I feel inside.

I keep trying to imagine how I'd feel if you told me that maybe it's best after all if we go our separate ways. I keep trying to think of how horrible that would feel and it makes me think that maybe it's not what I want, if it feels that bad to imagine you dumping me.

But I just can't take any more of this. I get closer to the edge all the time and I just don't know how I can go on keeping all of this bottled up inside me with no one but you to turn to and you're just not there when I need you. I can't even have a goddamn phone conversation when I'm so desperate to just talk about this and FUCK! HOW AM I SUPPOSED TO GO ON WITH THIS ?!

You say you were doing it for all of us, but did you ever once stop to think of how torn apart I would be if you got caught? Did you ever once consider how betrayed I would feel to find out all this stupid goddamn stuff about where you were and who you were with and what you were doing and how the hell am I ever supposed to trust you again?

I don't know if I can hold out waiting with all the shame and anger that comes with it, how THEY make me feel when I go there and how angry I get at being treated like they're better than me. I don't care anymore what you think of me or if you hate me for saying these things. Maybe you really don't care if I stay or not, maybe you really do love me *and it would be easier for you to get through this if you didn't have me to worry about, maybe all around it would be better if I just get the hell out and try TRY TRY TRY to FIND A LIFE AGAIN.*

When I lie awake at night, I wonder how I'm going to do it. Another three maybe five months before we even see each other face to face and then how long before we have sex? And then if we're lucky maybe we'll get to be alone once a month—or two or three months, for the next two years or three or ten. Goddamn it's depressing. I just don't know how I'm going to do it. It's been ten years since I've gone even this long without sex.

And what the hell do you mean by all this evolving stuff? Do you really think you're so evolved that it doesn't matter that you lied to me, hid stuff from me, and hung out with the disgusting people you "worked with"? How evolved does that look to you?

Are you so evolved that you don't need to consider what it does to me to think of how you convinced me to get back together with you and then promptly spent almost every night of the week, and certainly every weekend with your goddamn shitty friends in those goddamn shitty holes doing "business." I wish I had never heard about any of this, I wish I didn't know ANYTHING about any of it. The whole thing completely disgusts me.

And here I am now, still waiting for you, doing the snow fucking white like a fool and every time the thought of you in those places with those people comes to mind I see red and I just want to say the hell with it. He didn't think of me all those times, he didn't think of how hurt I'd be, or didn't care.

How could you want to keep secrets from me if you loved me ?

It's Sunday night and all weekend I've stayed home writing and painting and sewing and cleaning and anything else I can do to keep my mind off of everything else it's thinking. But it's no use. I think of how many times M. left me, how many promises he has broken and this choice he is asking me to make—this decision he seems to expect of me, how can he ask it of me? How can I ask it of myself?

The phone rings and it's my girlfriends insisting they are dragging me out, even if it's kicking and screaming. There's live jazz down the street and no cover charge and they are not taking "no" for an answer. Enough sulking already. Go get your face on, we'll be at your door in twenty minutes and you're coming with us, ready or not.

I grudgingly fix my hair, put on some makeup and miraculously, begin to feel better. Anticipating, even. Yes, I can have fun. And not feel guilty that he is sitting in a jail cell, a circumstance entirely of his own doing. I can go and listen to music and have a couple of drinks and a few laughs with my friends. Why not? The face in the mirror struggles to convince. The shades of doubt in my mind do not budge.

True to their promise, two friends are knocking at my door within twenty minutes and true to their threat, my coat is on my shoulders and I am fairly whisked down the stairs of my apartment, out the door and into the broad dusk of almost summer. Spring is still burgeoning and the air is green and juniper scented. I've been caved up all weekend and suddenly out here with laughing friends and jumping children and strolling couples I remember there is no alone except by choice.

Try, with a little help from my friends. Old song, good song. It remembers me.

We arrive and thrust ourselves into the tight little crowd that smothers the bar. The jazz is a sweet hum over the chatter and I sink into it and my cocktail, my favourite Dubonnet red on the rocks. My friends cluck on about this and that and content that I have permitted them to kidnap me from my self-imposed internment, they do not insist that I join in. I close my eyes and let the music wrap around me and the moment is a good one.

The evening is delightful. I laugh 'til my insides hurt, Hannah is in her finest form, recounting her latest encounters with the other species. I make her promise me she'll write a comic strip on the life of the single girl in the city. We start throwing around more story ideas, painfully true to life, too hilarious or humiliating to be made up and the three of us shriek together with laughter, oblivious to the stares from the men at the bar.

After a few drinks, my friends walk me home, the three of us linking arms. We are still laughing, unable to stop now, seized with fits of giggles like the teenagers we remember ourselves as, still can't believe we are not. Time has passed so quickly and fallen so hard on our shoulders. But laugh we must, laugh we will. The party has only just started. They leave me at the door with hugs and scoldings for any continued "pining" for M. I can still hear them cackling down the laneway by my house as I flip on the bathroom switch.

The mirror catches the briefest flash of a grin and it's gone. The image runs grey and cold, chiselled stone revealed beneath a mask of momentary comfort. In an instant, consolation is extinguished, dampened by the ready return of dark and fearful thoughts. Swollen with misery, the heavy heart returns.

I sit on the edge of the bathtub and let the familiar tide have its way. The sobs are deeper for the grief having been forgotten a few hours. I crawl into bed and bury my face in my pillow, weeping like a lost child.

JUNE 22, 19__

Dear W.,

It's Sunday night, around 6:00 p.m. I just called you—I was late and A. told me you went down to the bar for a drink. After your last letter, just hearing you went out to a bar kinda puts me in a, "Is this going to be the night" kind of mood.

Sweetie, please don't take anything I say to heart or feel that I am judging you in any way. You have absolutely every right to be angry at me and every right to be fed up with waiting for this to be over, waiting to see me, to be touched, to have sex, all of it. And I always knew it was just a matter of time before we would have the conversation we had yesterday and no matter how much you may sugar-coat it, the idea of you "having a friend" until we can be together just totally freaks me out.

I'm not trying to influence or manipulate any decision you may make. I know you feel like you are a victim of this whole thing, which was out of your control and in many ways you're right.

Regardless, I think I need to express my feelings about this. I know it can't be good for me to carry this around with me with everything else I'm trying to deal with at the same time. I don't know if what I feel is threatened or more hurt. It's kinda like a combination of both. I think you may have thought I would be able to hear this from you and deal with this because of all the past history and our other splits and how we both dated other people in between.

This is a lot different at least for me. At this point in my life (regardless of the bars), I have never felt a closer connection to anyone in my life. This time we aren't broken up, we are in fact talking seriously about marriage.

To hear you say, "I mean, I just don't think I can wait six more months, or a year, or whatever," creates a lot of fear and pain for me. It's a feeling of total helplessness. The fact is, I have absolutely no control over how long this takes. On the other hand, I feel like I'd better exert some control over it because if I don't, you'll just go out and get laid or find a new boyfriend or something.

Hearing this opens a floodgate of questions for me that I just can't answer, can't even comprehend, can't rationally even entertain. Just too many hard questions.

Is it fair for me to ask a beautiful woman, in her prime, to wait six months or longer for me?

If it is fair, what makes it fair?

Can I reasonably expect that I can consent or approve, give the okay to the person who says she loves me to have sex with someone else, without questioning her loyalty?

Is it a question of loyalty?

How could she do it if she loves me as much as she says she does?

How could I really consent if I love her?

If she had sex with someone once, would it by okay to do it again?

When you have sex with someone on a regular basis, don't you become attached?

Would it be fair for me to ask her to put herself in my position for five minutes and try to imagine what it feels like when your partner (the person you love more that anyone, the person you want to spend the rest of your life with) tells you she is going to make love to someone else?

Are there circumstances that make this okay?

Is it possible that she might find someone she could have really great sex with?

Could she fall in love with that person?

What if I told her I didn't approve?

Would she do it anyway?

Would she leave me?

Would she hide it from me?

When I call and find out she went out to a bar will I get any sleep that night?

If I were in an accident and couldn't perform anymore, what would that mean?

When your partner tells you of their intention to do this, if in fact things "take too long," is it normal for me to feel confused, frustrated, threatened, hurt, just crushed?

And of course, the final question for me has to be, will I be able to love and respect her as much if she does?

These are just a few of the millions of questions that have been bouncing around in my head ever since this came up.

The other day I saw a guy on my range looking really upset. I asked why, and he told me that he thought his wife was having an affair. I remember looking at him and feeling so sorry for him because he looked so empty, like his child had died or something. So we talked for awhile but he still didn't feel any better. During the conversation, when he asked, "Do you think your wife would ever do that to you?" In spite of wanting to spare his feelings, I immediately responded, "Not in a million years."

About twenty minutes ago he walked by my cell and asked who I was writing to. I turned to him and said, my wife. He must have seen the water in my eyes because then he asked if something was wrong and I just said, "Family problems." I was too embarrassed to admit the truth. I had been so certain the last time I had talked to him and all of that has disappeared. He said, "Ya, well yours can't be anywhere near the hell I'm going through." When he walked away the water in my eyes broke into tears. Yeah, me—tears!

Sweetie, PLEASE, PLEASE understand that I'm not just trying lay a guilt trip on you or anything. This is how I really feel about this issue and like we've been saying, if I learn anything from this whole mess it has to be the importance of expressing my feelings to you, especially about an issue that affects me so profoundly.

Frankly, I feel like I've fallen down hard and deep and the only person in the world that I trust has threatened to kick me in the face if I don't get up fast enough.

Next to my kids, I love you more than I will ever be able to love another single soul. And although I know this is a decision that you can only make on your own, it is necessary for me to express my disapproval as it may someday affect the quality or evolution of our relationship if I were to keep these feelings trapped inside.

It feels really good for me to have come to this conclusion. Although I recognize that my problem (being in here) is only temporary, I can't diminish the truth that I have been separated from my family (you) and have lost my freedom. So whether you do or don't go through with this, it makes me feel good to know that I made a decision that helps me to maintain my dignity. This renews my strength. That decision is, no, I do not approve of this and I do not believe that this will be healthy for the future of our relationship.

I know in my heart that I will never hold it against you that you entertained this idea. If you do go ahead with it, I promise that I will try as hard as I can to understand why and love you no matter what.

Miss you and love you more than ever,

M.

JUNE 27, 19__

Dear M.,

I got your letter and quite frankly, I was even more pissed off after I read it than I have been these past couple of weeks.

Like shit you don't want to guilt me out. Yeah, yeah, so NOW you want to express your feelings, blah, blah, blah.

And still, in spite of it all, I really DO know you that well that I can read between the lines and I know how really difficult it was for you to write that letter. I know it meant exposure for you and you would have rather "stuck pins in your eyes" as you love to say, than bare your soul to me that way. I know how much it would crush you to think of me being with anyone else.

And the truth is, I have absolutely, positively NO INTEREST in anyone else, in fact men seem totally gross to me right now. I just have so much anger over all of this and there's that nagging voice all the time that laughs at me for being such a fool. Sitting here waiting for you like a good little prison wife. Goddammit, it is such a pathetic picture and one that I never EVER EVER imagined for myself.

God I'm so tired of being alone and lonely. The worst thing is, I love to be alone, and when I'm alone and enjoying it I'm so happy. But being forced to be alone all the time, having no choice about it, is killing me. And it's ruined that happy to be alone feeling. I never feel very happy anymore, except when I'm talking to you.

So fine, I've heard you out, and maybe I am a fool but the voice inside is just going to have to learn to be ignored, because this little prison wife is gonna "stand by her man" (and the guitars rise to a crescendo and the twangy voice of Loretta Lynn fades into the night as I sit in front of the T.V. watching Seinfeld reruns and sublimating my sexual urges by digging through vats of Haagen Daz.)

Still love you, W.

JULY 10, 19__

Dear M.,

You've just called and the phones got cut off while you were in mid-sentence, and we've had a very upsetting discussion over the trial and everything. I know you're probably sitting there wishing you could call me and say something nice to make me feel better but here we are, stuck, with no possibility of communication.

And all I want to tell you is that you're right, why should you just jump at this deal, you're right to question your lawyer's motives, you're right to say why should you just take what they offer if it's not a fair offer and goddamn seven years sounds like forever. What if they're just giving us a line about the possibility of ten or fifteen? I mean, how do we really know?

I want to support you in doing what's best. I'm just scared and feeling like I just want this to start being over with, and I know you feel the same way but you're more patient about it. (Ironic isn't it?) But I also want to do what's best and not panic. And yet the risk of getting ten years?! Is it worth risking?

I guess I've just gotten again to the point where I'm so tired of eating, sleeping, living this thing day in day out. I never ever EVER can get away from it, it's always at least in the back of my mind and when it's not in the back of my mind, it's screamingly right in the front of my mind and all around me. And of course I know it is for you too, but you're living it and I'm supposed to be trying to carry on with MY life, such as it is. And if I don't carry on with my life then we aren't going to have a life together when this is all over.

I HAVE to get the mental and emotional space I need to stay strong, to not exhaust myself emotionally, to pace myself so that I can go the whole distance with this thing and not wear myself out emotionally before it's finally over. But I get so totally wrapped up in it to a point where every book I read is somehow connected, everything I buy or think of buying, every plan I make for tomorrow and many tomorrows from now, everything feels like it's tied in to this terrible ache of you being in there and us being apart. And right now at this moment I just wish to God there was some way to blank my mind out, to not have one single thought of this mess for even one hour, one blissful hour free of anxiety and hurt and depression and loneliness. One hour free from prison.

Love, W.

Chapter Seven

I go down to the water, book and straw mat I brought back from my trip to the sea, seems lifetimes ago.

The beach almost empty still, but for the occasional drifting of little clouds of activity from the west end, crowds beginning to gather there, popular spot even in the early of the day.

It's a clear-headed morning, jumped out of bed, quick before the thoughts could begin brewing, thick soup of woeful murmurings, rasping discordant my heart-strings. It is good, with sunlight, sand and other people's voices, solitary in my anonymity but not isolation. It is good to break this, my habit now to do.

God is here, in this moment, the spray of water and splashing sunlight on rocks and sand. God is here, childish voices, dogs and children running, colliding with Frisbees and each other; couples together, old friends walking, joggers pounding the boardwalk, it is good that I'm reminded that life still lives itself, with or without me.

I open the book... Virginia, she is to be savoured, almost line by line and so I read, I gaze, I drink in the sunlight that paints the tips of tiny waves; little lapping sounds of wavelets sliding in and out across stony sands. My mind is stilled on single thoughts, one at a time, strange to feel like this for so long it feels like years since my heart has been so still and not aching. Filling up again with sounds of other people laughing, some are dying too, I know that from the click of canes on the boardwalk behind me, step–click—step–click, we are all dying every day but still it is beautiful.

I slip into half-sleep, book in hand, lulled by the sounds of living.

God you are so full of surprise bouquets—so unfathomable, so unknowable. Just to be in your presence, it is a gift to be alone with you. The Tibetan gong goes off in my head and as I lose myself in the disappearing eddies of its tone I know the teaching—I am God.

July 11, 19__
Dear M.,

I was hoping you'd call tonight and I stayed in all night waiting to hear from you. I tried to get away from work to see you but I was just too busy to escape.

I can't shake this anxiety that you may think that I'm not doing enough for you. And it's EVERYTHING I can do just to get through an hour sometimes, just to not run screaming out into the street and get myself hit by a car just to have it over with. I get so frustrated when it sounds as though you are dissatisfied with what I'm doing, that somehow, no matter how hard I try to push myself beyond even my own depression and feelings of hopelessness, just to do what I can for you, it still isn't enough.

It's like a mountain falling on top of me, I just can't bear for you to think that I'm not doing enough for you or that I don't care enough. I know it's difficult—of course, it's hell in there for you but still, you had an opportunity to weigh the risks first. I didn't. And I would never have taken the risk because I would have known that it would take this much out of me. Anyway, I recognize that some part of me did choose it but that just doesn't seem to help at all in the dark moments.

Anyway what I wanted to share with you was the insights I just had in the midst of feeling this darkness and overwhelming hopelessness. The book I'm reading triggered this thought: that even though I'm feeling completely alone and unloved right now, and that's what makes all of this so hard, there is a reservoir—a "rainy day bank account" of love that people have for me, that I know about even though they don't show it very often or I don't feel it. I still know that it's there. My kids first of all, love me with all their hearts, I know that, even though they don't often show it and it's easy to forget that they love me, especially for them (to forget).

And my family, I know that deep down they really do love me even though they don't understand me at all. They still love me, as best they can. And of course you. I do know, really deep down no matter what doubts I battle with, I really do know that you truly, deeply love me, in as profound a way as anyone could love someone, the same way that I love you.

And so there's this little lake of love that I can picture myself swimming in and being revitalized by, even though I can't feel the love I do know, absolutely, that it's there. I think that's a really profound breakthrough for me, to have found this vision that I can call forth in my mind at these times of despair, and it will give me the strength I need to go on.

The second thing that came up in the midst of this was straight out of this same book. (I bought it today in the second-hand bookstore.) I've seen it lots of times, it's called Chicken Soup for the Soul and I've always resisted buying it 'cause it's made a big name for itself with the whole "touchy-feely" crowd and I didn't want to read more new age bullshit self-help "how to heal your inner child" shit 'cause I'm so sick of the commercialism that surrounds it. Anyway, it was cheap and I knew I really needed something to pull me out of this slump and so I bought it.

Well, I only read a couple of pages and already it gave me some incredible wisdom to draw on. One of the lines is "I knew in my bones that the love we give and receive is all that matters and all that is remembered (after death). Suffering disappears; love remains."

And it's so true. All that you and I will remember, when it all comes down to it, is the love that we have shared to get us through this terrible time. All that we'll remember in our last moments of life will be that we have truly and passionately loved each other. And nothing else will matter. Nothing else will be left behind but that memory of love. And that thought will get me through waiting out the day and the night until I can talk to you again and resolve these bad feelings between us.

Love, W.

July 22, 19__

I'm biting my lip while I push the buttons on the phone. It's still early and I call the lawyer at home wondering if he's up this early in the morning. It rings twice. He picks up and his voice is clear, businesslike. I say, "I hope it's not too late for me to be there. I mean, I've decided to come after all." There's silence while he takes a moment to recognize my voice. I clear my throat, determined not to let my voice waver, "I need to be there." He tells me to meet him outside of Court "J" at 9:30. M. needs to see me there, I think to myself, but I don't say so out loud. That's why I've decided to come. That's why I knew, when I finally slipped into sleep last night, that I would be there.

I'm there at 9:10, petrified of being moments too late and missing him. I'm wearing my favourite suit, the white linen, the one that needs to be dry-cleaned every time I wear it but it's so elegant, so sophisticated, so I save it for the special occasions. I take out the new white shoes I bought a month ago but haven't worn yet; they have an iridescent sheen to them and I admire them in the mirror, the design of the shoe is so perfect with the suit. I smile back at the image of the perfectly suited, shod and coiffed business woman looking out at me all glass and shining, radiant.

I'm pacing outside the locked courtroom and searching all the faces, the suits and the briefcases, no one looks familiar. I wonder if I'll recognize the lawyer, I've only met him twice. Then I see his face bobbing through the crowd that huddles in the hallway outside of Courtroom "J" and he looks like a saviour to me. He smiles and takes my arm and leads me down another hallway.

"Isn't this it?" I ask, pointing behind us to the huge oak doors of Courtroom "J."

"No, no, I just told you to meet me here because it's easy to find." He spoke quickly, to the point, but not gruff.

I feel a weird disappointment as I realize that the strangers I had been studying for the last twenty minutes would not be comrades. I had already invented my own stories for them, how they came to be there, which of them were "accused," which were victims, who was there as I was, out of love or out of duty or just curiosity. I leave them behind with their unknown stories and hurry with him up the huge stone steps. The lawyer asks me to sit outside another hearing room while he goes in and speaks to the judge.

"Can I see M.?" I ask, thinking he must be in the hearing room already.

"No, no he isn't here yet." He is rushed and impatient to go in, but he stops long enough to explain to me that we still don't actually have a hearing scheduled for today. We are only applying to the judge to hear the case, if he can fit it in, so that we will not have to go to court next week and have the case heard in a formal court where we would be taking our chances with the judge's decision on sentencing. We are asking for an informal hearing, during which the Crown and the defence will make a joint submission for a plea of guilty. We've already taken the deal for seven years, we just have to have a judge agree to it and make it official.

He is very patient in explaining and I know my eyes are wide and staring, but as soon as I hear "seven years" again, I have to strain to keep the tears back. I bite the inside of my lip, I dig my nails into the palms of my hands and open my eyes as wide as they can go. He asks if I understand and I nod that I do. He leaves me waiting outside while he goes in to request a hearing for a plea of guilty and a seven year sentence.

Twenty minutes later the huge door creaks open and the lawyer motions me to walk with him. I'm thinking we are on our way to another courtroom but he explains as we walk, me taking two strides to his one, that he has another case to go to right now, but the judge agreed to an informal hearing at noon today. It's now almost 10:30 and he asks if I can wait here until noon. I tell him I will go to work now and be back at noon because the courthouse is only a five minute walk from my office.

I thank him, though it seems an odd thing to thank someone for, but in that moment he is the only link between me and M., the only visible thread binding us and our future, our lives are literally in his hands. I need to like him. I need to make him a hero, even if only for the day, to get me through this.

Back at work I go about my usual duties as if there is nothing remarkable about today. Comments are made about my beautiful suit and my new shoes that I demurely accept. I laugh at the usual bits of office humour that are thrown about and concentrate on the tasks at hand, urgent letters to be typed and faxes to be sent and business to be carried out as usual. The surrealism of it makes me laugh in earnest and helps to keep me perversely cheerful. I feel as though I'm living a bizarre dream, acting out a role, sometimes it's light, sometimes dramatic but always just an act.

None of this could be real. I'll return afterwards and take up my work where I leave off, having just watched the man I love more than anything in the world, the man that I believe I came into life just to be with, being sentenced to seven years in prison, apart from me, apart from our life together.

And I will type and file and answer the phone. And it will be a dream.

Noon approaches and my heart starts to thump so I make myself breathe slow and deep and I pray my coffee won't come back up my throat. I feel as though at any moment I could suddenly fall involuntarily into some wild, irrational behaviour—hysterical laughter or heaving, sobbing tears or some huge vulgar burst of gastrointestinal discord that would completely destroy my cover of calm and imperturbable ordinariness. I even hum to myself, "Isn't it ironic..." and somehow I make it to the appointed time and I slip away back to the courthouse. "I might be a little late getting back." I tell the receptionist, just as natural as can be. "I have some errands." I feel so proud of myself, carrying it off so well, so smooth, I deserve an academy award (again) for this, I tell myself.

I feel calmer now, though my shaking hands don't appear to notice that I am calm. The lawyer meets me and we walk quickly together in silence to the hearing room. He smiles kindly at me as he opens the door and I feel like Alice stepping into the Mad Queen's Court.

The hearing room is about the size of a classroom, except for a very high ceiling, at least eighteen feet above us. Huge fans hang there and they turn lazily, pushing moist air around the room as it exits noisily from a vent high up near the front of the room. The room smells like leather and wood polish. Several rows of long wooden benches like church pews are lined along the back end of the room. We enter near the back, beside the first row of benches. Just in front of the first bench is a glass booth that runs half the length of the room. A smaller bench sits inside the booth; there is a two inch space between the glass and the back of the bench inside, barely enough room for a hand to slip through.

The lawyer indicates to me that I am to sit down on a bench and wait. I sit on the bench directly behind the glass booth. I sit only a few seconds and then I stand up again, it's impossible to sit still so I quietly pace, carefully placing one exquisitely clad foot in front of the other. I pace quietly, elegantly, a slow parading step, trying to even out my heartbeat. I remind myself that this is only a play and I am merely a player.

At the front of the hearing room stands an enormous oak desk, more like a throne, with microphones on it, and steps leading up to it. Behind either side of the judge's "throne" is a huge door. In front of the judge's area, but about two feet away from it (indicating "respect" I suppose) are two long tables, where the arresting cop and the two lawyers now stand discussing the terms of the "deal." I strain to hear them but their voices are almost lost in the vast ceiling and the noisy air vent and the glass between us that makes it impossible to hear anything distinctly. I want to step out from behind the glass to listen, but their seeming indifference to my presence is like a shield and I fear drawing their attention and losing the safety of invisibility.

I am expecting M. to be brought in through one of the doors behind the judge's desk and I pace with eyes glued first to one door, then the other. When he suddenly appears through the same door I had entered from, I have to catch my breath. This is the closest we've been to each other in six months, with no glass between us and I could reach my hand out and touch him if I dared. His hands are secured behind his back with handcuffs and he walks slowly but seemingly without effort, even though his ankles are shackled together. The shackles rattle and the sight and sound of them force a little gasp that I bite down and I command myself to *absolutely* not cry. M. has become used to the shackles, this is his fifth or sixth court appearance, in spite of his stated intention from the start to plead guilty to all counts.

A uniformed guard accompanies him and I am shocked at how young this guard looks. He can't be more than two years out of high school, I think to myself.

M. smiles wide the moment he sees me. My eyes sting from the tears I won't permit but I smile at him. I mouth the words "I love you." He says "You look great," very quietly and when the guard places him in the glass cubicle he points me to stand further to one side so that he can look at me. The look is warm and happy and wonderful. For one second we are suddenly alone in the courtroom and none of this is happening. We are simply the two of us, together, closer than we've ever been.

The rattle of the handcuffs being removed snaps reality back into focus. The shackles remain. Boldly, with the baby-faced guard watching my every move, I slip my hand through the space in the glass—it barely fits through, but with M's back against the glass I am actually touching him for the first time in six months. I can feel his warmth through his shirt, and he nods that he feels me too. It is precious and wonderful to be standing there with my hand resting against his body.

The guard's face goes pale when he sees me do it and he fidgets with his belt, his holster and gun attached to it like a useless afterthought. His expression reminds me of the child at school who is appointed to watch the other children while the teacher steps out of the room. Pumped up with self-importance the boy is torn between asserting his authority and fearing the sound of his own voice when it cracks out useless threats against the unheeding mob left in his care. In frustration and fear the boy stamps his foot and involuntarily he wets his pants. The other children fall about the room, hysterical at his misfortune and delighted at his mortification.

The boy-guard gestures to me to step away from the glass and I take my hand away, still feeling M's current running through my arm. "So you're the girlfriend, I guess," he says, his voice smug with unconcealed contempt. "He's going away for a long time."

"Oh, how original," I think to myself, but simply look away. He leans closer to me, getting bolder now that he has heard his voice out loud and it didn't crack and the lawyers haven't silenced him. Between clenched teeth, he says, "So, you think you're going to wait for him, do you? You won't be young anymore by the time he gets out." His voice is taunting, nauseating and he cocks his thin lips in a smirk, enjoying this moment of self-importance before a captive audience, a beautiful woman and her lover silenced and shackled next to us.

I ignore him and he boldly raises his voice a little louder, "I guess he should have been thinking of you when he did it." My eyes flash fire then and without taking a breath I freeze him to the spot with a stare that would melt granite. I am known for my stares. I know he can't look away, he can't move a muscle until I release him.

I let my eyes inch slowly down his torso, making a full stop at his crotch. My lips curl into a subtle sneer, serene amusement, an unspoken "and, is that all you got, son?" pricks his thin bubble of superiority. My eyes return to lock onto his and I can barely suppress laughter as he tries in vain to hide the sting of shock, injured pride, flashing across his face. He is once again the school-boy, wetting his pants in front of the other children. M. casts a glance at the boy-guard's red face and I see his shoulders shaking with silent laughter. He knows the kid just got "the look."

One of the big doors behind the judge's desk opens and he enters, a huge man, his gown unbuttoned and left casually open. He mounts the steps and seats himself on the great throne of a desk and everyone in the room stands still and silent. Court is in session.

The hearing is brief, fifteen minutes from start to finish. There are eleven counts in all, I am surprised as I hear them read aloud that there are laws against such things. Most of the charges are thrown in as bargaining chips to give the Crown more leverage. Out of eleven, seven are dismissed. Only three are important and he pleads guilty to all three. The judge hears out the lawyer's remarks and notes the unusual circumstances of the crime. Before passing sentence, he gives a little speech about how he believes the seven years to be very lenient in the case of bank robbery, with or without violence, but in this case he believes leniency is warranted. He hands down three consecutive sentences of seven years each. The five months already spent in the worst of all jails in the country is not counted. The seven years begins tomorrow.

The judge pronounces sentence and stands up. Everyone else in the room, including M., also stands and waits until the judge leaves. The guard rushes to replace the hand-cuffs, desperate to redeem his wounded dignity. M. leans towards me as he passes by me and again the guard recoils in shock and withered pride as we grab a fleeting kiss and smile at this tiny conspiracy. I fling one last look at the guard and my eyes are saying, "Yes, I would wait a hundred years for this man. And would anyone wait even a heartbeat for you?"

Leaving the courtroom, I hear him say to M., "She was in on it, wasn't she? She's as guilty as you are, I know it," and M's peal of laughter at this boy-guard's stupidity reaches me before the great door closes and drowns out the sound of shackles and footsteps and M's laughter fading down the corridor.

From W's Journal
AUGUST 2, 19__

It's done now. There's the last minute thing with the other lawyer, which really feels shitty, so rotten of him to manipulate us that way, but it's done now and for better or worse, it's over. Or at least, it has begun in earnest.

It did feel great, a huge relief afterwards just to have it over. We'll never know if the decision to take the deal was a good one or bad but at least the agony of not knowing is ended and he can get on with actually serving time. And life is taken off "hold" and moves on again.

Distance. It's wonderful. But it's always so much in the foreground of my thoughts. I really want even just a day of *complete* freedom. No thought of him or this nightmare or the heartache or any of it at all. Freedom. Peace. Separateness.

What would I be feeling now if he were not a part of my life?

That's what I need to focus on for awhile. There is where I'll find my healing, by focussing on myself, my own life apart from him, apart from "us," just me, who *I* am, what I am about. With all of this anxiety and trauma and things needing to be done all the time, calls to be made, letters to be written, it's as though every breath I take is focussed on him, on us, on being together again.

I feel like I need to breathe him out and breathe me in. I need to take a big break from the whole relationship and now, not being able to see him, or talk to him, or even write to him until I know where exactly he is, gives me the perfect opportunity to focus on reclaiming my life. And taking a good hard look at why I stay with it, asking the question "Why are the hard times so hard?" etc., is very healthy.

I need to take this step back and really examine what I'm doing in this relationship. I've stuck by him through the worst of it already so I don't need to feel disloyal if I choose to leave. And if this relationship really *is* for a lifetime, then it *will* hold up under scrutiny. I am not afraid to scrutinize it, to ask the difficult questions and even if I discover that it's not what I want, then I am not afraid to watch it crumble and walk away, if that is my path.

It's so healing to be here at the beach. The water splashing so gently against the rocks, it's like angel's voices. I feel my soul stretching to take it in.

A quote from an amazing book I'm reading, *When The Worst That Can Happen Already Has:* a young man, Derin McCoy, describes his spiritual awakening in the midst of assisting rescue workers pull victims, alive and dead, from the carnage of the San Francisco earthquake of 1990. He writes, "How long does it take a caterpillar to become a butterfly? It didn't take me any time at all. I had a metamorphosis right there at the bridge."

Well, my faith tells me that we will have a new beginning. That this is the new beginning for us. That my belief in him, in us, will not be wasted.

Chapter Eight

August 5, 19__
Dear W.,

Hi Sweetie, how are you? Well, here I am, in the Big House. I guess it's everything I had imagined it would be. But that will have to wait for another letter. This place is even noisier and busier than the Don Jail, if it can be imagined, and right now I only have a few minutes to write, before we go down for meals. The food is as bad here as at the Don, but there's more of it and I've learned to gulp it down without tasting it. I just stick to the vegetables—everyone says, don't trust the meat.

I know you've been worried ('cause I just know you), but I can't phone you until I get a "pin card" that is an encoded phone card with only approved phone numbers on it. So far, I have put only your number down because they gave me the forms to fill out before they gave me all my personal effects and so I didn't have either of my sisters' phone numbers (you know how I am at remembering numbers). Anyway, it takes a couple of weeks at least to get the numbers approved. I know you don't expect to speak to either of them, and I certainly do not expect it of you, but if they should happen to call and wonder where I am, please let them know that I can't call them until I get another form to get their phone numbers approved.

This whole place is about forms. I swear, hell must be a place where you spend eternity filling out forms for EVERYTHING including being allowed to take a piss. That's just about the only thing you don't need a form for here, and I'd say this is about the closest to hell that you can get, or at least the closest I ever hope to get.

So don't panic if you still haven't heard from me by the time you get this letter. I'm fine, everything's OK and you don't need to worry about me. Can't wait until we can talk.

Love you, M.

AUGUST 10, 19__

Dear M.,

When you told me, after the court hearing, that I looked so beautiful when you saw me standing there and you just couldn't believe how good I looked, I was so shocked. I mean, I had no idea you were thinking that at the time, you didn't let on at all, at least not in any way I could tell. Of course, you did say, "You look great," but it came out sounding almost obligatory. I mean, I didn't have to show up at all, I hadn't planned to be there but I went anyway, to be there for you. And you knew how hard it was for me to even come and so you had to show gratitude and so you said "You look great." I mean, that's the kind of comment I took it for.

But then I hear you tell me later how you thought I looked so beautiful and you told your cellmate how beautiful I looked. And I think to myself, "I really don't know this man. I missed it entirely. I didn't get that he really meant it."

And it just totally intrigues me to stay in this relationship to know you better. To someday know you inside out. To know your breath and how it feels to you. To know you and love you perfectly. Loving ANYONE perfectly has to be the most evolved thing that anyone can accomplish in this life. Except I think I already know you perfectly, if not completely.

I love you perfectly, if not completely.

I just don't know how to express what exactly I feel between us. I don't know if the words have been invented yet.

I want to be apart from this whole mess, the trauma, the angst, the anger. But I feel such a thread between us as if we're twins or something, completely inseparable no matter what the circumstances may be. It's as though the outside appearances, the everyday events of our lives are not real. The reality lies in what we FEEL, not in what we physically experience.

I've been reading this book about addiction to love and of course it has me poking and prodding at our relationship from every possible angle to ask the question, is it really love? I think the whole question of whether it's love or whether it's addiction is a matter of defining the relation between commitment and separateness. Yes, there can be separateness within commitment. And no, commitment does not mean melting into someone, conjoining. It means being separate and apart—together.

This is the lesson I keep getting from life, from us. Learning to stay separate and apart within a committed relationship.

Hard as it is, the forced separation, the impossibility of seeing or speaking to each other these past two weeks has been good for me, much as I hate to admit it. I feel cleansed. All the pain of the past weeks and months has finally come to mean something to me. I don't need to leave you to be separate from you. I don't need to change anything except my focus.

The focus is on ME now. Living for ME. Not for us, not for the future we'll have together, not for my kids, but for me. The perfect, in-God's-image being that I am, the being that chose this life. It's for me to live, to experience in it's fullest richness, even when that richness translates to suffering. I am grateful for it all, hard as it is. I thank whatever God there is. Life. It is good.

Love you, W.

From W's Journal

August 22, 19__

It's a quiet revolution within. My little girl has stopped hiding. I've stopped judging her and she has stopped running away from me. I've stopped blaming her, I have forgiven her and she has allowed me to comfort her, to hold her, to be her friend. I've never felt this before. It's awesome and wonderful.

I'm not the same person I was six months ago. I was close to the truth then, but now something definitely FEELS different. This time last year I had already come through so much. The bankruptcy, the relationship splitting up, having to start from scratch all over again. I had overcome so much. I felt exhausted, alone, beat up, confused, abandoned by "the universe," but still determined, persevering, still not giving up the faith in the rightness of my experience as long as I was being true to myself.

Now there's something new and it's VERY strong. I see no shadow of the helpless victim in me anymore. I see no Phoenix, either, rising from the flames. The rising has already occurred. It's a maturation of my faith and my strength. I don't feel the struggle today as I did then. I don't feel the plodding, getting nowhere. I don't feel fire, either, it's much more mellow than that. It's calm, mature. It's grown-up strength, real strength. Not hard strength like rock, but pliable, worked at, strong like sinew.

I don't feel all the questioning anymore, either—do I stay or do I leave? It doesn't seem to matter either way, because there *is* no addiction. There would be tremendous sadness if I chose to leave him, but the grief would go deep and then pass, without panic, without loss of *my* identity, without that terrifying, irrational fear of being erased.

Something has changed! Some bridge has been crossed and I have arrived safely on the other side. I've been carried, pushed, dragged. I've crawled, writhed, walked and even run at times. And now, some wonderful meadow of self-realization and acceptance of me by me has opened up before me. I step one foot into it, the ground is solid, the sunlight is real, the way home lies ahead.

SEPTEMBER 4, 19___
Dear W.,

> *Hi Sweetie, how are ya? I can't tell you how much I've missed you these past few weeks. I think about you every day and night.*
>
> *My little sister came to see me on Saturday, she showed up kind of late, so I only saw her for about 45 minutes. She was in town on her way to the U.S. for the weekend and I didn't know this before, but you get one visit before they've checked you out and given you clearance. But*

anyway, your clearance should be coming through any day now.

All in all it was a nice visit and I guess it gave me a chance to check out the visiting room. It's similar to the one at the Don Jail but there are chairs, like big ugly bar-stools, to sit on. There are also small glass partitions on each side of you, about ten inches deep, which make a kind a cubicle between you and the next person, and it blocks out some of the sound. That's on the visitor's side. On the prisoner's side it's a totally enclosed glass cubicle and we have to shut the iron grate behind us and lock ourselves in or you get thrown out of the visit room and your visit is cancelled.

Of course, I'm sorry to say, there is the usual glass partition between the inmates and the "outside world," but since you're sitting down you can get up closer to the glass and it feels a bit more intimate.

You don't use phones, instead there are small holes at the bottom of the glass between us, and these holes are supposed to carry the sound. Unfortunately, they are mostly blocked up with dirt and probably have never been cleaned out since the place was built, so you have to speak up pretty loud to be heard. And if the people next to you are loud, well then, you have to be louder. So much for privacy. I still think it's nuts that we can't have open visits.

I re-injured my back last week lifting weights and have been kinda laid-up. It's not as bad as the first time but it really pisses me off that I can't get any kind of medication, not even an aspirin, and I haven't been able to see a doctor yet. I spent two days flat on my back, unable to move even to get meals and all they did was come in to check that I wasn't stoned or dead.

Anyway, it's starting to feel better now and it may be for the best that I don't take anything that might depress me. But I sure do miss not having my beautiful W. around to spoon feed me when I'm sick. You've always taken such good care of me.

Well, I just wanted to drop you a line so you won't worry. I want to get this in the mail right away so it will get to you early next week sometime (they only pick up our mail on Thursdays). Can't wait to see you.

Love M.

(September 5, 19__, Street corner of Toronto)

"Breathe slowly. Breathe. You must catch your breath. Here, sit down on this ledge. Come, I'll sit beside you... (Somebody get a glass of water)... Come. We'll sit here so you can catch your breath. Big breaths. That's it. Breathe."

A woman's voice. French-Canadian accent. People running, too many voices, shouting. My own voice, babbling between sobs and panting. Can't catch my breath, it won't come in long ones, only quick short ones, the ragged ends of sobs. A glass of water is handed to me. I take a sip and immediately let go of it. It smashes to the pavement. I'm embarrassed. I start to cry again looking at the shattered glass, not understanding how it came to be there so suddenly.

"No police. NO POLICE!" I hear myself saying. I'm shaking, my voice is out of control, the whole thing is so strange like I'm watching a movie that's out of focus and the sound has gone bad.

A cop, short-sleeved uniform. Dark blue, not light blue like the guards. "Why no police, why didn't you want the police called?" but his voice is very kind. He is enquiring, not probing. The question is only a point of entry, an attempt to get past my locked up head, which will not let me speak, only cry and gasp in short, jagged breaths. Too many at a time. I am gulping air and I can't breathe.

"I need you to breathe slowly, now, breathe with me." It is him now asking me to breathe and he breathes with me and I am able to take a long breath, but the rapid-fire ones follow. We breathe together again. "Now, I need to know your name."

"Hate cops," between gaspy breaths, "Cops are... bad."

"Yes, I know you said no cops. Are you going to tell me your name? I'd like to help you. Can you tell me what happened to you?"

"I was walking. And then behind me... and... and my purse..." and the sobbing took over once again and the thought of my I.D. gone overwhelmed me and I became lost in great heaves of sobbing tears.

The cop was patient and kind. Perhaps my insistent distrust became a challenge to him. Whatever his reasons, he persevered past my protests and finally, broke through to the real reason for my distress. And my distrust.

"My I.D. It's gone and that means I can't see him tomorrow. I have no I.D. I was supposed to go and see him tomorrow."

"You were supposed to see someone tomorrow?" he echoed, trying to draw more from me. "So why can't you still see him. Who is this, your boyfriend, your husband, is it your brother you were going to see?"

"My... boyfriend. I mean, we're... c-c-c-ommon-law..." He was good at it. His voice never lost its kindness, never developed an edge of impatience or exasperation.

There were still a lot of people around. Someone had called an ambulance. I was mortally embarrassed and I knew I smelled like booze. I'd had three drinks and I felt fine when I left but now everything was out of focus. I wondered if maybe I was drunk and imagining all of this.

Someone spoke to the cop and explained that they saw a man—a young, black man, run from behind the building, across the street. Then he heard a woman yelling, and then he saw me emerge from behind the building. My leg and arm were bleeding. He turned back to see where the man had run and he was nowhere in sight.

So I wasn't just drunk and imagining it. I spoke to the cop. "I went out after work for a drink with the rest of the office." I began.

The bar was smoky and I was bored. I'd had a drink before we'd ordered food and I was starting to feel it. God, I just wasn't used to this scene anymore. Bodies and more bodies. I felt suddenly old, looking around at how young all these people looked, and these are the men and women running the country, carrying on business by day and look at what lost souls they are in the night-time hours.

The food arrived and I picked at it, I didn't have much of an appetite. Someone had ordered me another drink and I drank it automatically, without thinking, bored and looking around at me. The more I looked around the more I felt the crush of fear, some old familiarity about it. Fear? No, loneliness. The fear of being alone. It's everywhere.

Huddles of people everywhere trying to drown this fear of being alone. Being left alone, living alone, dying alone. Aloneness is a disease to them. Sitting there in the midst of it, I felt the infection start to creep over my skin: a slow-moving glacial tide, a creeping unstoppable, insatiable, greedy flood of cold fear.

On my third drink, I knew I'd had enough. Too many bodies, moving, jumping, reaching, grasping. Fear has turned to despair. I had to get out of there quickly, before despair had a chance to seize me. Despair is my own familiar disease.

I left the bar and began walking back to the parking garage. I should have taken a taxi, the thought pushed through as I walked crowded streets, the summer daylight just fading into dusk. I really shouldn't be driving, I thought. It's not only the drinks I've had, it's this infection, seeping, spreading. I feel the disease settling into my insides, creeping up through my throat where it sticks and I know then that it has found a foothold.

I glanced over my shoulder and up ahead and couldn't see a taxi. I crossed the street and then remembered, suddenly, that I would need my car early in the morning. Tomorrow I would drive to Kingston for the first time. The visits might be open, we don't know yet, but tomorrow is the day. We haven't seen each other, even through glass, for a month.

I have to be up at 5 a.m. to get there in time for 8:30 a.m. when the guardhouse opens. I was told if I didn't line up in time, I may not get in. My thoughts ran panicky now, Goddamn, why did I go out for drinks tonight, of all nights. Why didn't I just go home like I had planned.

I was so flattered that they'd asked me. I'd been working with these people for over six months and this was the first time they'd ever asked me to join them after work. I had thought I would have one drink and go home. I should have left after that first drink.

By this time I had reached the street next to the one my office building was on. The streets ran parallel, with three huge office towers separated by a pedestrian walkway. It was well-lit and I saw a couple sitting on a bench and two other people further along. A man and woman were walking alongside each other about a foot apart, probably worked together, they didn't look like a couple. Or maybe they were a couple who had quarrelled. Maybe they'd go home and not speak to each other all night and then she or he would turn to the other in the morning and the coldness would speak for itself.

I felt suddenly exhausted. The disease had taken hold. I needed to sit and think, to shake off this despair, this loneliness. The tears had started even before I felt the thud at my back and suddenly I was thrown to the ground. He reached and grabbed deftly at my purse but I was holding the strap and shouting, "NO! NO!" I wasn't thinking of anything but my I.D., my precious I.D. that was my only ticket to enter the prison tomorrow. In seconds the purse was out of my hands and he was gone, a light grey blur ahead of me.

I scrambled to my feet and tried to run after him. I was wearing a long skirt that day and I stumbled and tripped and fell again, hard, my chest hitting the ground. I opened my mouth to shout, "NO!!!" waiting for the sound of my voice, but none came out. The fall had knocked the wind out of me. I slowly rose to my feet and suddenly there were others shouting and people everywhere and all I could think of was my lost ticket to prison and no cops, please no cops.

"Hmm, So your boyfriend is in Kingston Pen. I see why you don't like cops. But we're not all bad you know." He had taken notes in his little pad while I told him what happened. Between sobs and tears and trying to catch my breath, he had the whole story, or as much as he needed.

"Your knee needs some attention, ma'am, and so does your arm. Does anything feel broken, can you move your arm okay?" I bent my arm and nodded. I was out of tears, the sobbing breaths were dry and exhausted me further. "Okay, but I think I'd like to get you to a hospital and just get you checked out okay? Is there anybody you need to call?" The tears run fresh again, there's no one to call, I cry to myself. No one to call. He's in prison and now I can't see him. There's no one.

And then I remembered the boys, only J. was going to his father's place tonight, A. wasn't going until Sunday. I should call my son at home. And a fresh insult hit me as I tried to remember my phone number and couldn't. I felt like an idiot. All I could remember was the first three numbers. I repeated them over and over to the cop. "244... 244... 244... 244..." I strained to remember more. He patiently waited for me to go on. "244..." and I began to cry again, more out of embarrassment than anything else. I felt foolish. Like I was bare naked and foolish and no one to call.

(SEPTEMBER 5, 19__ —INSIDE M'S CELL)

Attempts at sleep were useless, I had tried everything. It wasn't just the pain in my back either. Something else was nagging at me. Something bad.

I tried to shake it off, to make sense of it. It was that idiot guard who wouldn't let me get in line for laundry. All I had left to wear was a coverall I'd been wearing already for three days and W. would be here tomorrow. The visit would be behind glass, I found out. Maybe that was it. I was pissed off at finding out the visits still weren't open. *Why* weren't they open? The most hardened criminals in the country were housed on the other side of that concrete wall and they had open visits. They could hold their tattooed wives and touch and smell them. They could see their babies and not feel like caged animals. Why were we not allowed open visits?

I pulled and tugged at it some more and it stubbornly remained, a pulsing nagging thought of danger. I was accustomed to the smell of fear, it seeped from these walls like a black ooze, the reign of fear and greed and anger. But there was a drizzle of a different kind of fear pervading the usual storm tonight.

I worried about W. She was supposed to be driving the next morning, maybe she was going to have an accident and this was a warning, maybe I should call her and… goddamit, I realized that I couldn't call, the phones were closed and then the old frustration flared up and took over.

I was a caged animal, pacing, smoking, unable to keep still for a moment. I paced the full width of the cell—these ones were newer, wider, a full six paces wide and about ten deep. I shared it with only one other guy. He was a "rounder," been here before, knew all the ropes, but he was decent enough, in on solid charges—a drug deal gone bad. Legitimate charges, nothing involving innocent victims—kids, women, and he wasn't a rat either.

Those are ones you really come to despise. You're in here, you're the scourge of society and yet there's still someone lower than you, you're not down at the bottom of the food chain yet. No, down at the bottom you have the "diddlers and the rats" and eventually they'll get killed or nearly killed. If they make it into PC (protective custody) alive, some of them will make it back out to the street again but guaranteed, they'll get some of their own back, either in here or on the street. Nobody likes a diddler and everybody hates a rat.

My cell partner was neither, just a common drug-dealer and I could live with that. He was clean and kept his own business, which was a blessing, because the only thing worse than getting stuck in a cell with a diddler or a rat is getting trapped in with a guy whose gotta know *everything* about you. Except they don't usually come straight out with the questions, they just sort of sideways get in there, get all the information they can and then before you know it you realize this guy knows more about you than your own mother. Those guys are usually harmless enough, but they talk too much and knowing your business mixed with talking too much is a recipe for trouble.

My cellmate was usually quiet though, as I always was and so it was unnerving for him to see me in this state of agitation. I was getting low on cigarettes too, which could only mean I'd be on to his before long. And when your cellmate says "Ya gotta smoke, bud?" and he's obviously in a bad way, well, you really can't say no unless you want to sleep with your eyes open for the next six months. I was getting to that point of going off the edge and he could see it. He tried to talk to me, get me to watch T.V. with him, but it was useless.

Finally he switched off the T.V. and began pacing with me. Ordinarily, this would have made it worse, I would have pinned him to the wall and taken out my frustration on him. But somehow it felt comforting to have him there beside me, pace for pace, and it made me open up for the first time since I got there. I talked about W. and how much l loved her and how much she meant to me. As I talked a picture flashed through my mind of her lying stiff and motionless in the dark. I froze and began to shake. My cellmate thought I might be having an acid flashback or something. He started trying to "talk me down."

"No, man, it's not about drugs, man," I told him, trying to explain. "It's something... else." And there was no way to describe it, this chill of knowing something I didn't know, something bad.

I paced alone again for awhile—six paces left to right, ten paces, window to the bars—and finally jumped up onto the upper bunk and laid there while I smoked the last of my cigarettes, one after another.

I didn't even have to ask him for his, he just passed them up to me, "Here man, you need these more than I do."

"Look man," his voice went suddenly quiet.

I was deep inside my head by now and in the darkness his words drifted up to me like bubbles rising up through a still pool; they licked the surface and exploded into pinpricks of colour like the tiny lights on a Christmas tree.

"Hey, I'm sure she's okay. I mean, you guys, you sound like you really love each other and if there is a God, I mean, he needs all the help he can get right, to fix all the shit in the world. Hey man, I don't know if I believe in this stuff but, I remember at church, they told us, 'God is love.' If God is love, then you guys already have God happening right between ya's and your God just won't let anything happen to wreck it, man." He lay back on his bunk and took a long drag of his only cigarette.

"I mean it, man," he said, his voice trailing off. "Don't shake it so rough."

He was snoring a few moments afterwards, but the glow from his words remained. I had to trust that, whatever this feeling was, she would be alright.

Day took it's time in breaking.

From W's Journal

September 12, __

I keep wondering why the mugging happened, why did I bring such a thing into my life, why now? The irony is funny even to me, I mean here I was, about to go to prison to visit my convict lover and wham!

I get mugged the night before, my I.D. stolen, my purse and all its contents never recovered.

What am I supposed to learn from this? Why did this happen to me now? Was it retribution? Was it the gods saying, here you go, you want to stand in defence of criminals, here, see how it feels to be robbed. And yet that doesn't feel true to me, there's a hollowness about it that sounds too Catholic, so much like old tapes playing in my head.

Maybe I do need to know what it feels like to be a victim but not for retribution, the universe isn't getting even with me, it is providing experience to be used a fuel. Yes, I do know now, firsthand, what it feels like to be the target of random violence and robbery. Thank god it was only money he wanted, my mind is boggled by the idea of rape and what the effects must be for these women—and men, too, I guess, who are so violated at such a fundamental level. How do they ever recover?

I mean, here I am, it's been a whole week since it happened, and I'm still not myself. Something has been taken from me that's worth more than everything in my purse. I lost something precious. I lost my self-confidence, my assurance that I can look out for myself. For the first time, I feel fear when I go outside. I can't even think about going out at night, not even the few steps from my car to the house are worth the risk, the fear is too great. I know I only need some time to get over it but how do rape victims ever recover after so great a loss?

It doesn't help to be separated from M. and him so far away and can't help me in any way. He knew that night that something had happened to me. Paced all night he told me, drove his cellmate nearly mad, behaving like a crazed animal locked in its cage. He managed to get a call to me the next day, when I hadn't shown up and I could hear his relief when he heard my voice. I was ashamed at feeling some satisfaction, knowing he'd been worried about me, but I was more shocked at the fact that the connection between us really was that strong, that direct. It was as though we didn't really need any telephone lines if we needed to communicate.

But isn't that just what he's been telling me all along? "If you need me, just think of me, Sweetie, and I'll be right there. My spirit is always available to you." The power of the love between us never ceases to amaze me.

Sept. 15, 19___

Dear M.,

One of the side effects of this mugging thing is that I find it very difficult to concentrate and I can't read. None of the words mean anything to me. And T.V. is SO BORING, and I haven't felt much like writing. But when I got your letter today, I just had to write to tell you how much I love you and for you to absolutely put the thought out of your mind that I would leave you. Not now, not EVER!

I'm hoping to find someone to get some counselling from to get over this hump—it's a really terrible thing and it's shocking how much it can affect you even when you think you've gotten over it. But I think the stress just continues for awhile, and added to the stress I already have, it's not a good thing.

Love, W.

Chapter Nine

I wake up and expect it to be time, but when I raise my eyes to where I set the clock at the top of my bed, I'm surprised to see it's only 4 a.m. I don't have to be up until 5 a.m. The next hour is useless, I can't fall back to sleep. I'm so nervous and scared and excited, it's like it's the night before a big job interview or something.

I look at the clock again and the red lighted numbers tell me I have another half hour before I have to get up but it's useless trying to sleep anyway, so I get up the extra half hour early and I light the candles and bring them into the bathroom with me. I hate lights in the morning, especially this early in the morning and after such a restless, sleepless night. The shower is hot and good and it's great that it's so early 'cause my neighbours are still sound asleep and that means I won't have to compete for hot or cold water. So I stay in there just a bit longer 'cause it feels so good when the shower doesn't suddenly go boiling hot or freezing cold.

I brush my teeth in the dark and dry my hair and then finally, when I absolutely can't do anything more by candlelight, I resort to switching on the bathroom light, but I finish getting dressed in my bedroom with just the light from the bathroom streaming in so that I can see enough to put on some make-up and squeeze my contact lenses into my puffy eyes.

I cried a lot—all night, I think. Don't really understand why, just everything seemed to come up for me all at once, and it's been nothing but crying it seems ever since that mugging happened to me. All of this is so strange and new and in a way it feels a little bit like an adventure but mostly it's just terrifying.

I check my I.D. for the hundredth time. I was careful to already have everything in my purse last night and I even put my passport in there just in case. The night I got mugged I had been so panicked that I had forgotten all about my passport and that it would have been good enough to use for I.D. to have a visit. But as it turned out, I was in no condition to drive six hours or more to Kingston and back just the day after it happened, anyway.

I get in the car and I've brought along some tapes that I figure will be comforting and feel like company for the long drive. I have my map and I called the prison and got some basic directions on how to get from the highway to Millhaven. Funny how you never, ever in your life expect to have to be calling anyone to ask directions to a prison and if the people at the prison give you lousy directions then who do you call, the department of highways? "Yes, please, I'd like directions to the most notorious penitentiary in the country—well, no, it's not the most notorious, actually I hear it's really quite civilized compared to... hello?... hello?" I was so embarrassed to call around to the Bed & Breakfasts and ask how close they were to the prison and then they asked me, which one? God, I felt like an idiot. So, turns out there's about three or four prisons, plus a women's prison all clumped together there around Kingston. Seems it's the principle industry, i.e. employment of the district. Odd that they're still so stiff with you when you ask the questions and they know you're a prisoner's visitor. People are funny.

I get off the highway and head south like the guard told me over the phone. There's a sign that says Millhaven and I turn left off the highway and I drive way down past a bunch of houses and still nothing in sight that looks like a prison. So I stop to ask a girl. She looks about fourteen years old. She's standing down at the bottom of her driveway, I guess waiting for a ride from someone. When I ask if she knows where the prison is, she looks at me really strange and then shakes her head like she doesn't understand English. Well, maybe she doesn't, but she's red-haired and freckle-faced, what else would she speak, Gaelic maybe? So is prison a word you don't use with "decent" people around here?

Not daring to stop and knock on any doors, I figure I'm for sure on the wrong road and by now I'm panicking, 'cause M. told me that if you get there late they don't always let you in. And it's 8:30 already and they'll be opening the doors by now and what if I drive all this way and they don't let me have the visit? I have to go back to work tomorrow, I could only get this one day off.

I'm almost crying as I turn my car around and I hear the sound of gravel crunching hard under the tires and it reminds me of how hard we laughed at M's mother Bev, that last Christmas we spent together. Bev and M's sister Carol had arrived after a six–hour drive, with his sister just about foaming at the mouth, blaming her mother's driving that she nearly had a heart attack twenty times on the way. "Ah, you," Bev dismissed her with a languid wave of an arm. "I told you, it's just 'cause you don't have any *gravel experience*." Well, we all fell about the place, all except Carol of course, but I got to know his mother a little better on that visit and then I understood the comment to be vintage Bev. She was quite the character. He always told me, still tells me, there's no one in the world reminds him of his mother like I do.

Bev died three months after that visit. I know that was the beginning of M's unravelling. He just never got over it and never got over allowing the doctors and nurses to neglect her the way they did. She died of gangrene after an operation, when the doctors and nurses kept telling us she "just wasn't recovering" and they even tried to convince us that it was all in her head. Sent a shrink in to see her, instead of a surgeon.

The coroner said he couldn't believe it, how she could have been in the care of some of the most well-known surgeons in the country and they left her such a mess inside.

After that, M. was never the same, he never did keep a job for longer than a couple of months. And all he kept thinking about was finding some way to get rich quick, and one disastrous investment after another eventually cleaned us out. We had no money left, we had no hope left. Jobs were so scarce that we both had to swallow our pride and find work for minimum wage. I stuck it out, I think I'm stronger that way and the bottom line is, I had to provide for my kids. But his ex-wife had his kids and really I guess he was too depressed and too beaten and probably just grossly irresponsible as well and when our money ran out he just stopped making support payments. Stopped making any kind of payments to anyone. He just kept walking away, running away from all his responsibilities.

The road is ending now and finally a sign springs up that says "Millhaven Institution" and I turn the corner and even at the entrance I still can't see any buildings because of the way the driveway is built into an incline. All the buildings are only a single story high and spread out for a long way around. But as I drive to the top of the incline I can see it all vast and grey and strangely beautiful. There are a few lone trees scattered about, nothing big enough to hide in or behind, but lots of lush green grass and little garden patches crammed full of leaping reds and pinks and gleaming whites, all the more glorious for the greyness they punctuate.

I drag my eyes from the gardens and they are met with fences everywhere, spreading out across the lawns as far as I can see. At least twelve feet high is my guess, every one of them festooned with huge spirals of barbed wire, lest the gardens make us momentarily forgetful that we are now within the strict confines of prison security. I am surprised to find that the fences and the barbed wire cause me no distress, strike no terror into my heart, I am not suddenly tempted to turn the car around and flee screaming from the place. I continue up the long, climbing drive, the entire grounds now becoming visible to me.

The only structures of any height are the watchtowers—imposing grey concrete, the window panes painted red, mimicking the red-rimmed eyes of the wives and the mothers and daughters who daily file past underneath them. Silent towers, poised high above the ground like tight, giant fists holding vigilant guards inside, watching, waiting; they dominate the landscape, thrusting out from amongst the greyness of the flat prison buildings like the sharp pointed teeth that lie alongside a crocodile's tongue.

There are actually two prisons on this property, I learn from the signs, and I find my way through winding driveways to the one where he is being held in "Reception." The parking lot appears huge at first, and quite empty and I am delighted to think that my visit is assured with so few others here ahead of me. I soon realize my mistake as I come upon a small green sign with a drooping arrow, as though the sign itself has tired of announcing, "Visitors must park here."

The visitor's parking lot is tiny, with space enough for only about ten vehicles, perhaps twelve if they are tightly packed together, compared with the hundreds that can be parked comfortably in the staff parking lots on the other side of the paved roadway. The staff lot remains almost vacant and I remember it's still early. The day hasn't yet begun for most working people.

I squeeze my car in between two others and I'm thinking my heart is beating loud enough for the guards in the tower ahead of me to hear it. The day is exquisitely beautiful and as I walk away from my car I am surrounded by green lawns and gracious gardens: luscious bubble-gum blooms of rhododendron, their weighty heads nodding slowly back and forth as if shifting from foot to foot, idly biding time. Perfectly symmetrical row upon row of perky begonia, pink, white and red, stretch out glossy leaves, dew-dressed and stiff from the crisp of morning. Fat, contented giant impatiens take their shade under the trees, indifferent to the sharp blue whispers of the inquisitive periwinkle, stealthily peering between stiff cottonwoods whose impatient pink blossoms, barely visible, have already begun bulbing into the tight little berries of Fall.

I walk tentatively around the enormous concrete base of the watchtower, expecting at any moment to be addressed by the authority standing sentinel inside, large and terrifying in my imagination because of his concealment, like Dorothy's Wizard hiding behind great furls of smoke and the cunning that mirrors can conjure. But there is no giant hand upon my collar nor a voice booming out at my turned back as I hold my breath and push open the door of the gatehouse.

Inside, the concrete block walls are painted an institutional grey-green, tinted glass windows lining two whole sides of the tiny structure. There are others there already, one sitting on a grey-green plastic chair by the door, another standing by rows of metal lockers that take up another wall at one end, to the right of the door. The entire building is one room, dominated by a huge L-shaped counter, behind which is a small metal desk. The wall behind the desk is taken up mostly by a huge wooden shelf, split up into small cubby-holes, with names on plastic labels stuck to the narrow lip of each opening. The only other thing on the wall is a huge clock, so large that it reminds me of the clock that hung in the gymnasium at school, high above the basketball net; only this one isn't covered by a wire grill like the one that hung like a black, gauzy eyelid, over the gymnasium clock.

Around a small corner from the cubby-holed wall is a door, marked "Staff Only," with a grey metal chair beside it. The floors are painted grey concrete, like an unfinished basement and the scuffling of visitors' shoes bounce and echo off the concrete walls and floor and ceiling. Everything in the place appears slightly camouflaged, the monochromatic effect of the grey on green making it difficult to fix one's eyes on anything distinct, without an effort of concentration. Even the guard behind the desk is masked by the greyness of his uniform against the vaguery of the sameness surrounding him.

I stand in line behind the two other visitors who are waiting to sign in. Those of us waiting stand strangely silent, the way people usually are silent in church, even when there's no service going on. It is the silence of grave circumstances, serious events and sober contemplation.

Filling the half wall beside the metal detecting "doorway" is a huge sign, black letters on white background, with words like "not" and "must," in red paint jumping off the white background and further highlighted by italics and underscoring. The sign announces the rules of the prison regarding visits and states unequivocally the institution's measures for dealing with "contraband" and "disorderly behaviour."

The posted visiting hours have been changed at some time, evidenced by the yellowed vinyl label that covers the original numbers. The visiting hours are now 9 a.m. to 11:30 a.m. and 1 p.m. to 3:30 p.m. daily. "Visitors are **not** permitted to visit on two consecutive days of a weekend or statutory holiday. Visitors **must** be signed in before 9 a.m. in order to be permitted a morning visit and before 1 p.m. in order to be permitted an afternoon visit. The institution reserves the right to **cancel** or **suspend** visits for **any** reason..." It's my turn and I step up to the counter, as the grey-green guard pushes a clipboard crammed full of white, dog-eared sheets towards me.

"Hello, Ma'am, how are you this morning. New recruit? Here, give me an autograph, then," he says, tapping the clipboard with the end his pen. I stand staring at him, pen frozen in mid-air, I am unaccustomed to such familiarity and irreverent observance of the routine. I clear my throat, smiling, anxious to respond with the same casual nonchalance, and when I finally recover my voice there is no carefree, off-hand retort to slide off my tongue, only, "M-my husband just got here."

The guard chuckles and takes back the clipboard to examine "Visitor's Name" and the "Inmate's Name" I have penned in beside mine, and "Relationship," where I scribble "wife" for the first time. Before today, I have always written "girlfriend" and I feel a secret sense of pride in this bold new declaration.

It's only later I will realize that the guard is taking pleasure in this moment. This is his personal stage upon which he plays the lead role, a role that he creates as the mood suits him. He may choose to play it soft, with comedic devilry that brings a sigh of relief to the audience that stands before him, waiting in cautious silence, bound by the fear of reprisal, of tyranny, the fear of being forced to defend one's dignity despite the hard lump of terror that rises up in one's throat at the prospect of it. Or he may choose to assert his indisputable power, set the metal counter ringing with the slammed fist of authority that will send one's feeble plastic-coated identification flying across the concrete floor with the force of the impact.

Today, comedy wins out and I am confused but hugely relieved to see the mischief playing around the creases at his eyes as he quizzes me in a softly lilting local accent: How have I come to be here and why would I want to be indoors in such a crass place on such a glorious day? How is my husband's name pronounced and was I certain that I was in the right place? Uh-huh, and how long had he been here? Only a week, eh, and I was here banging on the gates to see him already, eh? Must be a fine fellow, to deserve all this attention.

He winks as he asks to see my I.D. peering at it with narrowed eyes as he holds it at arm's length, pretending to compare myself with the likeness in the photograph, mocking uncertainty as to its authenticity.

A big grin breaks over his face, the curtain draws, the production is ended and he resumes a kindly air of officialdom. "Well, ma'am, a fine fellow he may be, but unfortunately, there were a number of other fine fellows whose visitors got up out of bed a half hour earlier than yourself here, and that means I can't let you in past those gates until someone else has had enough and comes back out, or in an hour from now, whichever is soonest." The speech is quick and casual and has the ring of a thousand rehearsals.

"Oh." I don't know what else to say, I've just driven three and a half hours and now I am being told the visit will not be a mere two and a half hours, but a only one and a half hours and then it will be time to turn around and drive the three and a half hours back home. I am silent as I obediently go to sit and wait on the grey metal bench pulled up to a metal table that is bolted to the wall beside the lockers. The guard has given me a lock to lock up my personal effects, "Visitors are not permitted to bring any Articles into the Visit Room" the sign shouts, although I see one of the others clutching a small scribble pad and a pen in one hand. She is standing next to the lockers and I am surprised at how her carefully arranged hair, her subtle makeup and crisp summer dress don't fit the stereotypical prison wife and with a shock like cold water in my face, I remember once again that I too am a prison wife.

I put my purse and my sweater in the locker, but hold onto my I.D. as instructed. I also hold onto my book, which I open and try to read, but the play before me resumes and in spite of my hushed breath, wishing to sweep invisibly through this experience, I am once again a captive audience. The guard is addressing another newcomer, but he is turned in my direction and the wink of his eye tells me he is speaking for the benefit of both of us and so I listen, resistant but attentive.

"You need to get here by at least a quarter of the hour if you want to get in for the whole two and a half hours, ma'am. We open the gatehouse a half hour prior to the start of visiting hours and you can expect a line-up if you come here on a weekend. So it's best if you get here a little before that half hour prior and once you've signed in, you'll be sure to get your visit, even if it's shortened by an hour or so. You see, if you get here anytime past the first hour, then it's too late entirely and then you've got yourself up in the morning all for nothing, 'cause you can't get in. And here's a little advice for you, the afternoons are always the busiest and you can never be sure at all that you'll get in to see your loved one."

That would mean I had to be up at 4:30 a.m. in order to get dressed and drive the three and a half hours it took to drive here in time for the opening of the gatehouse doors. Either that, or come in the morning and wait 'til the afternoon shift opened and get signed in early. No matter how I did it, it would be a long day.

More visitors accumulate in the small room, the chairs in front of the window are all filled and another woman has seated herself beside me on the metal bench at the table. I sit as invisibly as I can and listen as the others trickle in, many of them local residents or coming from nearby towns, wanting to catch a quick visit in the last hour. I soak in the information sent ricocheting off the concrete walls, a chorus of voices, some barely a whisper, others loud and apparently not experiencing any gravity in this event, just another day in their otherwise normal lives. "Yes, I know there is a place you can stay, what's the name of it again, Charlene, what's the name of that place where the women can stay overnight?" "...It's about a $50.00 round trip, you know, so I don't make it too often..." "...Says he can't wait until he can wear his own clothes again, but I'm not sure how..." "Well, they told me that there's this form you have to fill out...." Snatches of worthy information that I log and catalogue and make a mental note to investigate further.

I sit silently, not daring to ask questions, gripped by an irrational fear that tells me that shattering my invisible wall of silence would mean exposure and rejection, turned away at the gates with no visit, no sight of him. The first hour passes quicker than I expect as I sit with glazed eyes fixed on the pages of my book, imitating reading. Other visitors are returning from their visit after an hour, and I am struck by the thought of leaving before you have to, so accustomed have I become to draining each visit of every second of allotted time, drinking in each moment I have with him like a precious elixir. It has been almost a month since we laid eyes on each other. The thought makes my eyes sting and I blink them hard and stand up, turning to re-open the locker and I stuff my book inside with unnecessary deliberation, surreptitiously flicking the annoying tears that have pooled into bulbous drops at the bottom of my eyes.

I watch the clock slowly peel away the 90 minutes left of our visit, one jarring second at a time. It is time to go inside.

Each visitor must first walk through the metal detector that looks like a regular metal door frame like the kind you see in airports, and then a few steps further and you're through another glass door and outside the back of the tiny building. If the metal frame doorway beeps when you go through it, the guard might pass a black stick perfunctorily over your clothes, which apparently assures him you are not smuggling any weapons into the institution.

We arrange ourselves loosely in single file and I count my breath slowly in and out, forcing myself to not run ahead, seeing it's useless anyway, as the guard in the little building we've just left waits until we are all gathered up past the first huge iron gate, which clangs shut before he pushes the button to open the next one. A few feet ahead and up some stone steps, the building lies waiting with my lover inside in anxious anticipation. He knows I am coming today. My heart is beating so fast now, I can't even count my breath but still I move my feet slowly, in time with the others, though I'm desperate to rush past them in my haste.

I lift my face to the sky, suddenly remembering the sun's glory and I feel it warm for a last brief moment before I am swallowed by the great doors, the sound of the grinding gates of the penitentiary closing behind me.

I admonish myself for shaking as I hand yet another grey guard my I.D. and state my inmate lover's name. They punch my raspy response into the computer and I hold my breath while I wait to learn my fate. "Alright, you can go in," is the terse response and I wait obediently until they buzz open first one enormous iron door, and when we are all collected tightly between two such doors, the first door buzzes locked and a second door buzzes unlocked. We are permitted to enter the confines of the visit room.

The visiting area is divided into two parts, one side for "open" visits and the other with a row of the glassed-in cubicles that M. had described to me in his letter. I pass through to the area designated for "closed" visits with only a brief glance at the other side where blue-jeaned men and women sit on high stools at tables bolted to the floor. Children sit and play beside them on worn and dirty orange carpeting, sparse and threadbare, everything orange and brown, the interior obviously not updated since the orange and brown days of the early seventies.

I install myself in an empty cubicle near the far end and while I wait for him to join me, I clear away the empty pop can left by a previous visitor and brush the spilled ashes onto the floor. Inside the cubicle, on the visitors' side, there is a small orange counter top, stretching the width of the unit, about two feet, and about a foot deep. It's made of melamine that hasn't been wiped down in ages and I try not to think of the germs as I gingerly put my elbows on it and lean into the smudgy glass, breathing too fast now, my quelled impatience beginning to collect into a pool of barely subdued panic.

Our 90 minutes together has become 75 minutes and I tap my fingers softly on the orange melamine, on the glass, on my leg, it's now 65 minutes and the panic is a river rising in my throat and I look over beseechingly at the guards in their office behind the glass. I know they have seen me anxiously watching the clock though they have expertly avoided meeting my gaze. They share a joke amongst themselves and I imagine the idle patter they amuse themselves with through dull and dragging hours, melting into days and years of the same listless boredom.

The rage rises up now and it's my own actions I fear, I repeat over and over to myself, "Soon, he'll be here soon" like a mantra. Finally I can stand it no longer. I emerge from the cubicle and plant myself in front of the big glass window like a starving street urchin, wet nose pressed against the window of a fine restaurant. They look over at me as I stand before them, jabbing a stiff finger in the direction of the big clock behind them and the tears have begun to roll down my cheeks, fat and deliberate and I can do nothing now to hold them back.

I stand there at the mercy of these stone-coloured men and the younger of them, thin, with a pinched-looking mouth and red-veined nostrils finally picks up the receiver of the phone on his desk and makes a call. He nods at me to go back and sit down and moments later, I see M's head come through the big iron door on the prisoner's side and he stands on tip-toe to find me, standing and waving to him, sobbing now, not caring that the others hear me or what they think. His head bobs past the grates locked behind other visiting inmates and he slides smiling into the cubicle on the other side of the glass.

His smile instantly vanishes when he sees my tears and he asks what's wrong. Through the glass and choking on my sobs, I point to the clock and say weakly, blubbering, "Only an hour, we have only an hour," and he shushes me, his hand on the glass as though to smooth the creases in my forehead and brush away the tears, "Shush, Sweetie, it's okay, we have a whole hour, Sweetie," and his smile has returned and it's infectious and my tears are suddenly joyful and sweet, the sound of his voice fading all fear and drowning my rage and washing away, at least for the moment, the crushing weight of my helplessness.

SEPT. 25, 19__

Dear W.,

> *Hi Sweetie-pie, it's Monday afternoon and I'm just sitting here thinking of how great it was to see you on the weekend so I thought I'd drop you a few lines. I spent the morning out in the yard playing hand-ball and tennis. It was a beautiful day outside, I got lots of sun. Had a few laughs with one of the guys as well.*
>
> *But hopefully, it's back to business tomorrow. I still have to do the lifestyles and substance abuse questionnaires (more like "Inquisitions") the last two segments of my orientation. Then I will be ready for classifi-cation. I sent a "Kite" (memo; brief written message; communication by letter) to C.R. She will be the person to assign me a Classification Officer when I have completed all of my orientation programs. I requested that she check my file to see how I am progressing as far as placement is concerned. I told her I am very anxious to be classified. Trying to get my name etched in their minds—it's the only way to get things done, somehow rise above this vast sea of people that have to be herded, tagged and catalogued, much like the branding of beef or shearing of sheep. It really begins to feel like that too, like we're just a herd of animals being dispatched with as little human involvement as possible.*
>
> *I put in all the requests that we had talked about at our visit. Between responses to those (hopefully they'll respond!) and finishing up my orienta-tion I should have a pretty eventful week. I just love getting out of this dingy and dismal cell. The ceilings are so low and the lighting is very dim, not like the glaring bright lights at the Don Jail. It really feels like a cave or something here, and if we don't get out in the daytime for awhile—they usually only let us out at night—it begins to feel like I'm living under-ground. It's very weird and it fucks up your thinking, I mean, you start thinking like some underground creature, a mole or a rat or something.*

I have put in about five or six job applications. Anything to get out of this cell. Also, because of my back, the doctor said that the worst thing for me to do is to sit or to lie around. If they don't put me to work there's nothing else I can do BUT sit or lie around. Usually you have to wait over two months (sorry to say, Sweetie, I could get stuck in this hole for up to six months) for a job but the John Howard Society guy that you sent to visit me said he would try to put in the "Patch" (use political influence to manipulate a decision; put in a good word; pull a few strings) for me because of my medical condition. Worth a try!

Well, my beautiful (pleasant to the eye; very attractive; how my Sweetie-Pie looks; W.), I don't really have any more news. Except of course that I love you more and more every day, but that's old news.

Bye for now, Love ya, M.

SEPTEMBER *30, 19___*

Dear M.,

I'm trying to write every day like I promised, but it's so hard. These two-minute phone calls really suck!! There's no time to discuss anything, to exchange any news, it's total BULLSHIT!!!!

I'm really tired and I still have so much to get done tonight, so this is gonna be a short letter. I've written to the MP's offices to thank them for their help (they made some calls to try and get your paperwork going) and I'll send you copies of those letters in my next letter, but I know you want me to get this in the mail tonight so I won't wait for the photocopies.

J. didn't get into that great school and so I've got miles and miles of red tape and bullshit to deal with again. I'm thinking it would be better to keep him out of school altogether rather than throw him to the wolves in the zoo they call the public school system. Drugs, crime, violence—what the hell is a kid supposed to learn from that? I really don't know what to do with him. He just can't go to these other schools where he's one of 1200 or 1800 other kids, 40 kids to a classroom, it's

*hopeless, he doesn't stand a chance. Needless to say I'm pretty strung
out about it. God, I am so tired of fighting for EVERYTHING!!!!*

*I wish so much we could even get decent PHONE TIME together.
God how I hate this disgusting system and the power tripping. How small
a person do you have to be to get satisfaction from stomping on other
people's personal rights and freedoms? How are they any better than the
criminals they despise? I wonder how they sleep at night. It's sick that
they feed off the powerlessness of people in prison—and their families,
all of us wives and mothers and whatever—in order to put food in their
own mouths. And they so get off on the power. Disgusting pigs. Strange
what makes some men (and women!) feel like men. Enough of that.*

*The MP's office says it's not supposed to take more than eight weeks
for your assessment and she's going to follow up with it. I hope she
means it. The sooner you get placed, the sooner we can have open visits
and hopefully, if you're moved closer, I'll be able to come every week
again. You know I will if there's any way that I can.*

*I'm sending some stuff in this letter—the phone numbers are impor-
tant, but if you lose them, I'll have copies. John Howard Society will
accept collect calls, but they're only open 8:30–4:00. I'll be calling
tomorrow to follow up with them and I'll advise them that you may have
difficulty contacting them. Queen's Legal Aid is also on this phone list.
That's who you call for a lawyer. And of course, the Tourist Bureau
will have invaluable information for you on the many exciting sites of
interest in the Kingston and Millhaven area! Don't miss this opportunity!*

That's all for now.
LOVE YOU SO-O-O-O-O-O-O MUCH!! W.

Chapter Ten

OCTOBER 10, 19__

Dear W.,

Sweetie, we've just got off the phone and you sound upset that we just don't have enough communication. I know how hard these unscheduled phone calls are, and they're frustrating for me too. But you know that if it was my choice I would sit and talk to you forever. Of course, you wouldn't like the phone bill, but it is impossible to explain to you how difficult it is to get phone time here. I'm just not in a position where I want to piss anyone off.

I want to explain why I haven't been writing so often because I think not hearing from me has added to your frustration. I hope it doesn't sound like I'm just making excuses but I know if you could live a day in my life you would definitely understand.

I wake up at 5:30 a.m. to be at work for 5:45. By the time we have finished cooking and serving breakfast and cleaning the kitchen it's 9:00 a.m. This is always the busiest time of the day. I take a shower, sweep and mop the cell, if I have laundry I battle my way into the line to wait for the washing machine. By then its usually almost 11:00 a.m. and it's time to start serving lunch. Back again in my cell at around 1:45 p.m., I'm off again until about 3:30 p.m. when it'll be time to get ready for dinner. During this "time off" it's IMPOSSIBLE to do ANYTHING! The noise on this work range can be heard throughout this whole jail. And it's a very tense, threatening noise, very difficult to describe to someone *who's never experienced it before. Things are going on here that I can't write about or talk about on the phone and everyone is buzzing around in a kind of nervous haste. Guys are in and out of your cell every five minutes, for—seemingly—no particular reason.*

Everyone is busy trying to drown out the sound of someone else's radio with their own; 30 different T.V.s, tuned in on 30 different stations have to become background noise while you try your best to concentrate so you can read or write. Alarms, the P.A. system, voices in every shade of tone and volume from whispers to growls to shouts completely surround you at every moment.

I would like to try to take a nap at this time because I never sleep at night anymore, but only a fool would lie down in his bunk and close his eyes with that much commotion going on around him. (Perfect case in point—it's now after dinner and I started this letter this morning). It's taken me all day to write—on my day off—only about one and a half pages.

Anyway, my point is that it's not as simple as getting a letter from you and sitting down and writing back. Especially when I need to put so much thought into it. Twenty-two hour lock-up was great for writing but coming to this work range is going from one extreme to another. But rest assured that a week shall not pass that you will not receive at least two letters from me from this day forward. Sometimes I don't get back from work until 7 p.m. or even later and the cells are all open until 10:30 p.m. By that time I'm ready to collapse. Which is right about where I'm at now. Sweetie, I'm sorry but it's past 11 p.m. and if I don't get some sleep I'll be in sorry shape tomorrow.

Remember how much I love you.

Love, M.

MP OPPOSES PRISON T.V.s

A Reform MP wants to pull the plug on prison T.V. privileges.

Art Hanger also says federal prisoners should not be paid for work they do in prison.

"I suggest they work for free because they sure took enough from society in the first place," Mr. Hanger said yesterday.

He asked Solicitor-General Herbert Gray to remove all television sets from federal institutions, saying prisoners are "sitting on their duff" watching cable at taxpayers' expense.

Mr. Gray acknowledged that the Correctional Service pays half of the cable bill, but told Mr. Hanger prisoners should have to pay by 1997."

The Daily News
October 6, 19___

OCTOBER 12, 19___

Dear M.,

I've been trying to sleep for the last three hours and everything just keeps rattling around inside my head. I probably won't end up sending you this letter, although I really wish you could know somehow how really afraid I am of being hurt by you even more.

Everyone in my life has either deserted me or betrayed me. Not because they have something against me but because it seems to be human nature to do so. I find it all so discouraging and impossible. My family, my friends, people like N. who I really believed was a true friend. And all I keep thinking of is what if you do the same things to me that you've done before—run away, refuse to deal with problems, refuse to communicate with me and work things out? It's your nature to run.

The truth is, I want nothing more than to wait here, to be steadfast, faithful, come and see you every chance I get, do everything I can to help get you through this, and get me through this, but I just can't shake the idea that you will betray me again the way you have before. This habit you have of walking away when things get tough... You see what happens when you don't clear things up, they just come back to haunt you at a time when you really need to believe that you're on sound footing.

Do you realize what it would do to me if I were to wait for you and stand by you through this whole thing and then six months after you get out you get another wild idea in your head and you take off to chase some other dream or fantasy or get-rich-quick scheme, god knows? I mean we were only back together three months this time and things were okay, but I hardly ever got to see you and I made a lot of allowances for you being sick and everything. What's it really going to be like when you get out? No one's going to wave some magic wand and make all the everyday badness of life go away for us. How will we deal with those kinds of problems when we didn't deal with them well before?

How can I know that this time it really is forever?

Love, W.

*O*CTOBER *19, 19____*
Dear Sweetie,

Just got your letter and I'm glad that you had the courage to send it to me. No, it's not pleasant to get bad news or even hear bad things from you given my present situation, but like you say, life for you goes on and if it is to go on for us together I need to address the issues of the past that I never properly dealt with. And it is my own fault that you are having these doubts and fears now because of my past behaviour and how I never wanted to deal with difficulties between us before.

Even before I got your letter, I've been spending a lot of time thinking about the future, about our future and it brings up a lot of sad memories for me. I think of the past and the present, of all the heartaches I caused you. In fact, aside from the few really good periods and the laughs we had together, most of my memories of the last seven years seem to be of difficult times, hardship and struggle. Even sadder for me is the fact that most of those hard times were the after-effects of my irresponsible ways, i.e. risking it all, making poor choices, and quitting things before I even gave them a chance to work.

In fact, I can't honestly recall ever finishing anything I started—businesses I launched, educational programs I started, good jobs I left to chase some get-rich-quick-scheme and even walking out on our relationship when the water got too hot. You are right about all these things and you have every right to bring them up now, when I am asking, or wanting you to do the hardest thing you've ever done before.

And thinking back on all of it, the one clear thing that stands out in all of it is that no matter how bad I messed up you always stood by me. You always had faith in me, in us. Blind faith and unconditional love. The only thing you ever asked in return was that I act responsibly and that I love you back. Well, there's never been any question about the fact that I have always loved you, but WOW! have I made some really bad choices! And that brings me back to my (or our) present situation.

Here I am paying the ultimate price (my freedom) for the most reckless thing I ever did in my life (which ironically happens to be one of the only "projects" I completed), and there you are again. Not only paying the price with me but helping me to get through it. W., you've responded far beyond the "call of duty."

Being in jail has definitely made me realize things that I had not realized before. One of those things is the other or new reasons why I love you so much. Ironically, one of those reasons is exactly what I used to hate about you. I used to see your practicality as weakness and I hated that. But you weren't weak, you aren't weak, you're very practical and that's good. That's very good. In fact, I've learned through all of this that you're one of the strongest people I ever met. You're stronger than me in many ways and that surprises me every time I think of it. No matter what happens to you or what circumstances you face, no matter how bleak the story gets, you get through it and come up smelling like a fucking rose.

After all the crazy schemes I've tried over the years to finally find myself here, you're still right there as strong as ever and that really does surprise me. Not that you're crazy to be there, but that you're really that strong. After all the shit you've been through in the last eight months you're still right fucking there. Even in your weakest moments when you're depressed and frustrated and you feel like you just can't take any more of this, you still answer that phone and accept the charges every time I call. You're still waiting there and you still tell me how much you love me.

Given our history, I honestly can't say that I have ever met a more courageous person than you. I don't think that even you realize how strong you are. Yes, you are also very sensitive, which makes it even more amazing that you have stayed so strong through it all.

Being in here hasn't made me mature any faster, but it sure has helped me to get to know you in ways that I may never have, if I had not come here. And of course that makes me think of the meditation session I had at the Don. "This was a necessary step in the evolution of your relationship." In my heart I really believe that.

I know you tell me how weak and discouraged you get sometimes. If you ever feel it's too hard on you please don't let anything compromise your emotional or financial stability. In fact, if you walked away from this tomorrow, I would probably still be amazed that you stayed as long as you did. I think I would remember you as a hero.

If you don't walk away, if you decide to stick it out for the duration, I can promise you all of your efforts and faith will not have been in vain. I feel I owe you something far more valuable than my own life. I owe you a wonderful life for YOU, with many years of happy memories and you shall have them!

I have always had lots of determination but I have lacked in discipline and integrity. It's a shame that I had to fall so deep to finally get such a clear and vivid view of the big picture. A shame that I had to be reduced to the life of a convict to finally identify the things that are truly important in my life. But now that I have seen and understood, I am making a decision that these are the things I must work towards and I will have them.

I guess my whole point is that I realize how much pain I have caused you in the past years and I think I understand what you are going through now. You give new meaning to the phrase, "I'd stick by you through anything." If you allow me, I'll spend the rest of my life making you a happy woman. Making us happy together.

Only one word can describe the love that I feel for you. PERFECT.

And I'll tell you as many times as you want to hear it, if that's what makes you happy. Remember, we are connected. This time will end and we will be happy.

Love you perfectly, M.

October 27, 19___

Dear M.,

Just got your beautiful letter. I've read it three times and went back and read the others too. And the beautiful envelope you made! I'll treasure that forever.

M., I'm so sorry for having made this so much harder for you. I wish I could have been a rock and not have caused you so much worry and anxiety. This has been a terrible experience for me, it's true, but my lessons are coming through it too, and although I wouldn't in a million years choose to do this (although of course we both know on some level I have made that choice), I am grateful for all the learning and growing I have done as a result of the pain and struggle.

Seeing in your own handwriting the idea of me giving up on you and leaving you, made me cry. It was good to get the acknowledgement from you that you understand how hard it gets sometimes and how I feel like I just won't make it through another day. But leave you!!!! It's unthinkable. Utterly unthinkable.

You and I have become so close we are inseparable. Like you said, time and space can't separate us. I feel you around me all the time and at times I know you are sending me love or your thoughts. This is only a test of our love and loyalty and we have both passed the test with flying colours. Nothing will ever tear us apart now.

This support group you told me about has been great. I think the people there are really sincere although I feel almost as though being part of it steeps me even more in "prison life"—hey, good title for an article—A Day in the Life of A Prison Wife—ha, ha. Anyway, speaking of writing, I'm putting together a newsletter for the group and all the inmates in the prisons they visit will be invited to submit articles, poems, etc. You can too! And never mind articles, where's my letters? You've fallen w-a-a-a-y behind!

I feel stronger now that I've at least been able to see you again. The drive was very exhausting and it's was so hard to wait so long and then get such a short visit. But all the way home I kept saying, "It was worth every minute. I'd do it all again even for ten minutes."

Love you and I'll see you soon! W.

P.S.—I'm sending manila envelopes and a book of ten stamps—and some photo's, and a copy of E's reference letter in case you need it.

N*OVEMBER* 2, 19__

Dear M.,

This morning I woke up and said, Today I want to forget all about PRISON for a whole day. Not possible though. I knew this would be the last chance I'll get for awhile to get the group's newsletter done, 'cause next week I'm on the AVP—Against Violence Program—all weekend. This week has been totally hectic with getting J. into a school and buying them both new clothes and shoes and... ($170.00 for J's shoes!!). Anyway, that's all done now and hopefully this week will be a little more sane for me.

Anyway, as for forgetting all about Prison today, that was impossible because of course my phone rang all day from inmates at the Don Jail who have heard about my work with the support group and the newsletter. Glenn and Mark say Hi! Mark is doing really well, he's been moved to Brampton and has been there three weeks. He'll get out in April next year. His family comes to see him (they have one-hour open visits there!) and he says that there's lots of rules that must be obeyed but there's no locked doors and there's a really excellent system of settling disputes. It sounds very human, unlike what you are suffering through.

As I told you on the phone, the news is not good for getting trans-ferred. I'm furious and I feel, once again, beaten by the system but hopefully I'll get somewhere with my meetings this week with the MP. I certainly don't want to stir up any shit, I just want your court documents sent out and for the process to be completed in due course. It's what we should be able to expect of the system and these unnecessary delays only make family support more difficult and how the hell do they expect rehabilitation to work? Or do they give a damn? Cathy, from the MP's office, said that the person she spoke to at Millhaven was quite reasonable and sympathetic and so on, but apparently you still have to have the "risks" part of the assessment done and she said that could take another eight weeks. But the bottom line is, they don't have to process you until eight weeks after they get the court docs, so as long as the clock isn't ticking for them, why get on it?

I don't know how much effect my efforts will have but I'm doing the best I can. It's a fine line between doing things so that I don't feel so helpless and consumed by the system and sitting back and waiting so that I don't exhaust myself emotionally and physically by running all around town meeting with this person and that person and making endless phone calls and writing letters, etc. I'm trying to keep a balance so I don't just discourage myself with not seeing any results.

The newsletter so far looks great, I'll put a copy of it in with this letter, but it's not finished yet. I should be able to get it out for next week, though. I'm hoping to get up there to see you next weekend but I'll only get the one visit and I really need to see how I feel, but you know that if I'm up to it I'll be there, for sure. I miss you so much and not being able to talk properly on the phone is so discouraging. The only way we can talk is by letter or visits so I really will try to keep up the visits.

I'm doing my best with letters but you just wouldn't believe how much work it's been just doing what I've been doing (writing letters to MP's, etc.) and still trying to keep up with work and life in general. So honestly, I'm doing the best I can and I'm sorry for not writing more often. But needless to say I never stop thinking of you for a moment.

I talked to the managing director of Prison Life Magazine *today. It sounds like a great publication, he's going to send me a couple of issues. It's run and written totally by inmates and ex-offenders (he himself is* "an ex-con" as he puts it). He was in "the Bay" and he says it's not that bad, but he hasn't been there for four years. He says there's a good computer program there too, and he says he got transferred to a camp from there pretty easily (I forget how long). So I'll try not to get too discouraged.

But this waiting and not knowing how long before we have open visits is so unnecessary. I get upset every time I think about it. But November will pass and at least we'll see each other for Christmas, unless they think of some other obstacle to throw at us or a new hoop we have to jump just so they can stay on top. God how I hate this system and the abuses it fosters.

I know there's so much more to say but I'm so tired and I've been sitting at this computer now for about seven hours (other than phone calls from prison!), so I really need a break. I'm back to work tomorrow, so much for a day off. I promise to write again soon.

Love, W.

NOVEMBER 3, 19___

Dear W.,

Sorry I haven't written sooner. With all the excitement around here and my somewhat less than usually optimistic attitude, I've been feeling kinda withdrawn the past couple weeks. I was really hoping to talk to you last night 'cause I missed you on Thursday. Hope I catch you tomorrow. Tell A. I'm sorry I had to cut him off like that last night, but there was guard right behind me and he barked at me to "get off the phone and back to your cell." Whenever there is an outbreak of violence of any kind anywhere in this institution, everyone gets locked up right away.

Last night, the residents of "J-Unit" (the range that houses inmates who have been charged with committing crimes WHILE incarcerated, i.e. stabbing another inmate, smuggling drugs, etc.—the inmates of "J-Unit" do not leave), refused to come in from Yard and hell kinda broke loose. They burned everything in the Yard, were going over internal fences, just being "J-Unit" I guess. I mean, hell, they're already doing

Life, what have they got to lose? Anyway, the noise kept me up 'til 4:30 a.m. and then all the cells facing the Yard were emptied because guys were helping "J-Unit" by throwing them stuff from their cells. We got sent to the cells across the hall until this afternoon when they finally got "J-Unit" back to their cells. What a drag, four of us crammed into one tiny cell.

This all started 'cause two days ago they found some kid dead in his cell. He started out at Kingston Pen (K.P.) doing eight years for rape when somehow he got hold of a female clerk, took her hostage and raped her. Got 25 more years and got sent here, to "J-Unit." Day one, dead. We haven't had Yard since all this shit started. I guess they need time to rebuild the Yard, now. I heard a rumour that there may be a hole in the fence somewhere so for sure we won't get Yard 'til everything gets fixed up. What a place. Anyway, the fun's over 'til next time.

NEXT DAY.

I'm starting to feel better again. I did my "lifestyles" program last week so that makes my orientation program complete. As soon as they get all the paperwork in, I can get classified and out of here. Going to check first thing tomorrow to see if I have a Classification Officer (C.O.) yet.

I hope you're feeling better, Sweetie-pie. I'm sorry if I have been pressing you to write. You take your time and get back to me when you feel relaxed and well-rested from now on. Don't write because you feel obligated just because I wrote to you. Shit, it's been tough for me lately, and I don't have a fraction of the stresses you have. I'm sorry I've been so pushy. It's just that I can't wait to hear from you. Ha! the poor mailman. He's literally scared to come on the range now, if he doesn't have mail for me.

Well, Sweetie, my hand is getting tired and I'm feeling kinda brain-dead so I'm going to sign off for now. I'll write again in a couple of days.

Love ya, M.

November 14, 19__
Dear M.,

Hi Sweetie—Haven't heard from you all weekend—guess your phone time got screwed up. I hope that's all it is. I always worry about you with the shit that goes on in there, riots, etc. I really hope everything's OK.

Well this is the end of week four of the new breathing exercises and I still can't get over the miraculous improvement! I am 100 percent me and 100 percent happy. God I really hope this is the key I've been looking for to deal with my emotional ups and downs.

You know it's really taught me something, these last few months where I've "lost myself." I hadn't realized how much I had grown to really like myself, to enjoy my own company and to respect my view of the world and life. I am really quite amazing. For instance, today it was such a beautiful day, so warm, not a hint of winter in the air. I waited 'til 2 p.m. and finally decided you probably weren't going to call (don't worry, I used my time very well, planting some mums on the deck and cleaning up and stuff) and so I went down to the beach and it was very very windy.

But what an amazing feeling. I felt so much a part of the wind and the waves and the sunlight. It didn't feel like there was any ending to me and beginning of the rest of the universe. It was so serene and peaceful and it didn't last long but it was enough of a glimpse of who I really am inside. I really respect my connection with the Universe and that feeling of being part of the whole. The energy that makes up my body is the same energy as what makes up the water and the sand and the rocks and everything. I really felt it and basked in it.

These are the simple joys I have that make me so happy and so appreciative of being who I am. I missed these joys and the happiness that I had really come to feel. I'm so happy to have it back and I only hope I can hold onto it this time and not lose it. It was the mugging that threw me off and hopefully now I've managed to regain that peace of mind that it took from me.

Oh—oooo—I had to stop typing cause a bug just flew up my nose.
Yech. Don't you HATE it when that happens?!
So bye for now, can't wait to hear from you—love you as much as ever!! W.

From W's Journal

4 A.M., SOMETIME IN THE MONTH OF NOVEMBER.

I'm sleepy, not clear in the head, and you beat like a drum in my head and keep me awake through the night. I close my eyes and you're still there like the image that's burned in behind the eye after staring too long at a thing. It's an image of us I see there, you holding me, us stretched out together on the sofa, the big cushions of it thrown back behind us.

And then another image, like it's superimposed on top of the other and it's me alone, in the candy-cane striped terry robe you bought for me two Christmases ago: I'm hugging it around me and I'm stretched out alone on the sofa, the cushions don't need to be thrown back 'cause it's only me, by myself. It's sometime very late in the night, very early in the morning, the time of sleep for everyone else but me. I come out to the sofa to stretch out, somewhere at least other than my bed where I toss and turn and get sick over thinking of you in that horrible place. It's two weeks since your arrest and every night I wander out to the living room in my candy-cane terry robe, hugging it around me as though it was you, it is a comfort.

I half-watch the last bits of a late late movie, my vision blurred through half-tears, not fully cried they sit between my eyelids, plump but not full enough yet to slide down onto the stripey sleeve of the candy-cane robe. I drop my eyelids, letting the tears cry themselves. They feel cool, not warm, tickling softly down my cheeks, I don't brush them away. I keep my eyelids closed tight on the tears, my sobs fade into a whimper, I shrink down inside my candy-cane shell, and allow myself to sleep at last.

The image fades.

And now, here I am awake again at that wee/late hour between the night and day. It's long past summer now, the nights are cooling into frostiness. My terry robe is lying across my bed, I sleep with it on top of me like a teddy bear, still a comfort because it reminds me of you. I sleep through most nights now, at least it's not still the waiting, the not knowing, the time-stretching-out-forever feeling of dread and doom.

I close my eyes this time too and again I see it, the image of us, you holding me, your arms wrapped around from behind me. You kiss me at my temple, you stroke my hair.

We haven't touched in ten months.

I never would have believed how starved for your touch I would become. My children sometimes hug me, occasionally I'll allow a friend to hug me hello or good-bye, maybe even a kiss on the cheek if they catch me unaware.

It's easier to not be touched at all, because none of it is you. I can't believe this ache, it's physical, this longing, this grief, it's physical. I understand the way that someone dies of grief. I understand and know what you mean when you say that if I die before you, you'll be only days or hours behind. I think, though, I'll linger on, if you go first. I'll linger on in a blissful kind of heartache with closed eyes that have imprinted on them the thousands of embraces we'll have shared 'til then, all of them stained like sepia prints into the deep brown shadows that lie behind my eyes.

Chapter Eleven

December *8, 19*__

Dear M.,

I missed your call tonight. I was so disappointed I cried for hours. Then I looked at all the (handful) of pictures I have of you and I read all your letters again and I remembered once more why I'm still here. Sometimes I just don't know how I'm going to get through this—three years, four years, everybody (ex-insiders) says you won't get paroled after a third, but then they don't know you and don't know how much you don't belong there, and I have to keep hoping for the best.

I just keep coming back to the fact that I really truly love you and I want to spend the rest of my life with you. And this test of the relationship seems like a heavy price to pay but once it's all over it will be behind us forever and we can move forward. I know that once we're able to start our lives together again the past will really be the past and I'll forget all about what I'm experiencing now. It's just getting there that scares me. Sometimes it's just a huge wall that I can't see around or over and I just feel so helpless.

The kicker is, I was feeling so good today. All weekend in fact, I've been getting some really powerful insights. I've been feeling so fat and gross and old looking lately and so I really dug into that and looked at the reason why women always seem to need men's approval and why our appearance is such a big deal.

Why do women rely so heavily on what men think of them (i.e. how attractive they are) for they own sense of well-being and self-appreciation? And I figured it out. It all boils down to instinct—in the pack or the tribe the woman depends on the man to go out and hunt for food and to protect her and the children from danger. Her life depends on how much a man values her. And in the pack mentality, the only value is in being able to produce offspring, so of course, sexuality is the only trump card that a woman's got. So naturally, being the preferred sexual object is critical to her security and even her life. And so even removed from all of that tribe stuff our instincts tell us that if a man doesn't find us pleasing, then no one will take care of us. So we'll die.

The thing to get is, how do you get that sense of security and "being taken care of" or protected, without needing it from outside of ourselves? How do I give it to myself so that I never have to go looking for it from someone else, never have to depend on anyone else for it again? That part I haven't got yet and maybe it'll be awhile but I'm working on it. In the meantime I still feel really fat and gross and ugly. I hope it passes.

It sounds really terrible in there—locked up all day and showers every two days. It's inhuman, they treat you like you're a bunch of animals, they really want to just lock you all up and forget about you but keep the big money machine going and padding their fat pockets at your expense. They don't give a goddam about rehabilitation.

I mean what about the guys who aren't like you, who really are weak and easily influenced but maybe aren't bad guys so much, just kinda lost? What hope do they have for coming away from this experience with any hope for making a new life? Of course they find themselves right back in there again, they don't have life skills, they don't understand why they do the things they do and they don't know how to examine their lives.

The system simply perpetuates itself and the guys running things are making a living off it so it's in their best interest to keep it going, to keep these guys circulating in the system. It's truly sick. I really believe that if the general public knew more of the truth of how the system works and how badly inmates and their families are treated, more would be done to change things. I don't know how that gets started and I don't want to be the one to start making waves. I just want us to keep our heads down and get through this but then if everyone thinks that way, nothing will ever be done to improve it. It's a catch-22.

What they don't understand is that they haven't just sentenced the offender, they've sentenced his whole family. Just because someone you love commits a crime doesn't mean you should have to suffer with things like insufficient communication—this whole telephone thing is absolutely disgusting, it's got nothing to do with taking your freedom away, it's forcing you into complete silence, cutting you off from everyone on the outside. This is absolutely barbaric and what's more, it's counter-productive.

Cutting an inmate off from the only hope he has—his family and friends—guarantees this guy will not be able to turn away from his life of hopelessness, helplessness and crime. Why should he care about what he does to other people? Why SHOULD he examine his motives and thoughts and develop a sense of compassion or empathy for his fellow man? Why wouldn't he hate the world after he's lost everything? You can't live in a vacuum. If there's no love or caring going into a person's life, then there's none going to come out. Is this not logical and apparent to this useless fat bunch of bureaucrats?

Sorry to end on this note, Sweetie, I'll climb off my soap box now.

Love you, W.

I arrive at the apartment around 6:30 p.m. Dinner was to have started at 6:00 and I'm embarrassed to be late but how do I explain how hard I had to fight myself to be here? I had been invited, weeks before, by my dear friend Sandra. She had been one of the first I had told and typically, she had offered her sympathy, prayers and tremendous compassion. Sandra understood shame and fear and how these can make prisoners of us all. She knew M., though not well, and her acquaintance with him had been during our very worst times, when he ran out on me at the first sign of trouble.

But none of this altered her compassion for me when I finally had the courage to tell her the truth. I had been so anxious that her response would be judgmental and harsh against M., given all the times she knew he'd left me crying, while he ran from our problems, from us, from himself. But instead I found only love, an embracing quality of caring and empathy that were almost more than I could bear, gracefully. I declined numerous invitations to join her and her friends and preferred the comfort of anonymity, the safety of isolation over the security of companionship.

But she persisted. And it was, after all, Christmas.

The prisons are closed for two days at Christmas. The irony slapped me in the face every time I thought of it. People are in prison, their families miss them most this time of year, but on Christmas Day and Boxing Day, no visits. And phone calls are almost impossible. I had thought of going up for Christmas Eve but it fell on a Tuesday, which meant asking for a day off work again and driving back home for three and a half hours, right in the middle of snowstorm country. And it would be dark long before I got home. I hated night driving in a snowstorm. Anyway, M. wouldn't hear of it, what if I hit black ice and my car went off the road in that deserted stretch of highway... and on and on. So he phoned me early on Christmas Eve morning, when he could be sure to get a phone and we made the best of the visit behind glass the weekend before Christmas.

I had been invited to join other friends for Christmas dinner; it seemed there was no shortage of invitations for a solitary woman, perhaps because I had become so scarce of late. Many of my friends knew about M. by now. Some had been shocked; others were a little intrigued. But no one condemned me, although occasionally a comment would drop that would betray their underlying reproach.

I still hadn't gotten up the courage to tell my family. At best, my parents tolerated the fact that M. was in and out of my life. They blamed him, perhaps rightly, for the financial difficulties I had suffered through the past five years. M's name was pretty much unmentionable with my mother, but I would mention him just the same and my mother would act like she hadn't heard me and then change the subject. I couldn't imagine their reaction if they knew the truth. Still, this was Christmas and in spite of myself I missed being with my family who were all so far from me.

I missed having a family altogether, since I always encouraged my boys' choice of spending Christmas with their father's huge family. Why should they miss out on all of this? It was their birthright. I tried so hard not to feel self-righteous about being alone but in spite of myself there was a hint of heroism in letting them go.

Which was in the end what decided my choice for me—staying home alone on Christmas Day was simply indulgent martyrdom for its own sake and not to be tolerated. "I *vant* to be alone"—fooey! It only works for Hollywood. You have no right to sit home alone and feel sorry for yourself. You have wonderful friends and friends of friends who want you to come out and enjoy! Celebrate! Bah humbug! The chatter in my head prattled on endlessly as I dressed, did my hair, *forced* myself to put on make-up—yes, you are going *out*, you *will* make an effort and you *will* feel good about yourself... my "nurturer" voice had adopted a distinctly Nazi tone.

And so at 6:30 p.m. I arrived, casserole in hand, smile glued to my face and surprisingly, after awhile the smile became real and natural and it didn't hurt a bit.

Dinner was casual and wonderful and the warmth of these new faces and their excited conversations should have lifted my spirits. It could have done, but I was determined to pine. How could I enjoy myself, apart from him at Christmas? In spite of my constant internal scolding my melancholy clung to me like a security blanket and during the brief prayer ceremony, I fully indulged it, basked in the grief of this longing and separation.

But there's next year, maybe a pass to come home and, I promised myself, every year after.

I said my good-byes early, determinedly sad, and climbed into my car—safe from any watching eyes I let the tears go. I didn't know if the tears were more of sadness or of anger at myself for allowing such indulgence, but I knew going home to an empty house was out of the question.

I drove first to Rosedale, where my Aunt Eva had once worked as a housekeeper, a neighbourhood that defined for me and carried all my childhood Cinderella dreams of wealth, prosperity and living happily ever after. The homes on these streets were stately, elegant, though much smaller than I remembered them. They had seemed such sprawling mansions to a little girl from the suburbs.

Trees between snow-draped lawns were graciously festooned with lights; glittering gold and silver trim caught the glimmer of starlight and Christmas displays. Enthusiastic hobbyists had fashioned Father Christmas and reindeer in lights to join the festivities. Stars and snowflakes and luminescent garlands lit the Christmas night like a Broadway opening.

I left the light show and drove toward the lake, the Beach, to watch a light show of another sort.

I was thrilled when I stepped out of my car and saw that the night was clear. As clear as it ever was, in the city. And stars could be seen, the milky way, I thought I could almost see it. Not as spectacular a show as in the mountains of Arizona, where I'd stood fascinated only months before, gazing at Hail-Bop cutting a glorious path for audiences the world over. But this was my night sky, my little corner of the universe.

I stepped closer to the water, crunching over crusty mounds of snow and frozen froths of sand sealed over with an icy glaze. The waves were gentle, but somewhere farther off I could hear them crashing like some distant laughter in celebration of this mystical, glorious, this holy night.

Closer to the water I left the lights behind and in the inky darkness I prayed. The sadness had disappeared, I stood there with my angels and with God and with M. and we all embraced, full of joy at this moment, at the sheer magic of being together in all of it. The wind blew past me and I didn't feel it cold as it circled me and then, with a flick of its mighty cloak, it lifted a corner of the darkness where I could gaze beyond into the light of many futures, many pasts and know that it is all one.

The distant waves cease their laughter for a moment and begin to sing softly,

> *Row, row, row your boat gently down the stream*
> *Merrily, merrily, merrily, merrily*
> *Life is but a dream . . .*

My voice is drawn into the merriment, *Life is but a dream...* and then, from under the waves, from behind the night sky, drifting up from the rocks and battered bits of driftwood, M's voice joins softly with mine, *Life is but a dream... Life is but a dream...*

MILLHAVEN PRISONERS RIOT

Rioting inmates at the Millhaven prison near Kingston returned to their cells peacefully late yesterday after a tense stand-off at the maximum security institution. The disturbance began in the afternoon when 27 prisoners used broken furniture to smash their way out of three rooms where they were being held during a cell search. Guards used tear gas in an attempt to force them back into their cells. An emergency response team was called in from nearby Kingston Penitentiary and eventually persuaded the inmates to return to their cells peacefully, said... a Corrections Canada spokesman.

The Daily News
February 6, 19___

The heat in the kitchen is thick and wet and the smells are heavier even than in the ranges. Smells of meals from days and weeks gone past hang thickly in the air and cling to every surface, stuck to the ceiling fans like the grey dust that has crusted to the fan blades and gripped the tops of the cupboards. The stainless steel hasn't been cleaned in months and the grilles are cleaned only by virtue of the high heat. The grease is pushed over to the edges and builds up until it is finally scraped off onto the floor where a dirty mop will pass over it at the end of the day. Meanwhile, working at the grille, I try to watch where I step, not wanting to track smears of thick black grease into my cell when I leave.

I toss the frozen patties of meat onto the grille and they sizzle as they slide across the surface, skidding to a stop when they hit the resistance of the grease. I'm reminded of the frozen cow dung we used to throw at each other as kids, skimming them like little flying saucers over the heaped tops of snow forts. These "burgers" don't look much more appetizing than the cow dung missiles, but they're government approved, real meat and they're one of the better meals served at Millhaven. There's not a lot that can be done to desecrate burgers, at least not compared with the chicken-a-la-king that's usually served at the end of the week, using up the leftovers.

I've come by this kitchen job by a sheer stroke of fortune, the riots in "J-Unit" having necessitated a complete lock-down of the range. "J-Unit's" meals still have to be prepared and served while they are locked down 24 hours a day but the threat of being caught in the midst of rioting means that the regular kitchen staff are temporarily relieved of their duties. Even inmates can't be forced into doing work that could endanger their lives.

So when word got out that they were looking for volunteers to cook for "J-Unit," I was there with bells on. I didn't care how dangerous it was, I needed to get out of my cell and working before I started a riot of my own. And so far, it had turned out to be a good situation for me; I could prepare my own food, simple but decent, avoiding the horrible slop that was forced on us, the most inedible mush you could ever imagine. The Chinese and Vietnamese cooks in the kitchen were all "lifers" but they took a liking to me and they could cook up a storm. Eating well was picking up my spirits and my health had already improved in the few days I had been working here. The threat of rioting didn't even phase me.

The burgers were almost done but I knew I would be ordered to flip them again and again until they were cooked brown-black beyond all hope of good eating. Salt and pepper were never used, so everything was tasteless, or worse, it all tasted the same. Bland, greasy, overcooked.

Somebody mentioned that the kitchen was to be sprayed for cockroaches today, but when the guy arrives with the tank full of roach spray and starts spraying in the midst of food preparation, I am stunned. I shout, "Whoa, hold on a minute, you can't spray in here now, there's food cooking." The guy just looks at me and laughs, and then the kitchen supervisor comes in and gives me a look that tells me to shut the fuck up unless I want that tank of spray shoved up my ass. "Cook the goddamn food, that's what you're here for," he growls while the sprayer, grinning, carries on spraying all around me and overtop of me, covering the grilles and the burgers alike with the pungent poison that is mixed double strength to combat the virulent cockroaches that breed in this filthy place. It makes no difference how much poison they use, the place is so infested that no amount of spraying has any real effect.

What happens next is something right out of a Stephen King movie and I watch horrified and helpless, thinking *"The riots didn't scare me, but this I wasn't prepared for,"* as swarms of cockroaches seep from every crevice, driven from their hiding places by the force of the poison spray. They drop all around me, and I step away from the cupboards as they drop onto the floor and the grille where the burgers are still sizzling. I hear little pops and crackles as the roaches first hit the burning surface and then, seared by the hot grease, they fry into hard little lumps. Little licks of fire burst up and all around the cont-aminated meat and sacs full of eggs are released by the horde of dying insects, scattered like confetti over the grille, the floor, the food.

I stand open-mouthed, thinking out loud, *"Well, I guess this food is garbage,"* when in stomps the kitchen supervisor, bristling and snarly at being forced to work with an amateur. He gives me the look, the one that says where the hell do I think I am anyway, this ain't no McDonald's, asshole, and without batting an eye, he yanks the spatula from my hand, deftly flicking fried cockroaches off the still spluttering meat, from the grille onto the floor. He accomplishes this quickly, with the practised expertise of an artist and soon all that remains on the grille are the hissing, hard discs of meat, although scattered all over the grille and on the burgers are tiny black crisps and it's impossible to discern whether they are tiny lumps of meat broken away from the patties or the egg sacks that the roaches dropped in their last moments. Like exclamation marks, the little bits of gristle that one is accustomed to finding in the meat become suspect, they look too similar to egg sacs, same colour, same texture, who would know the difference? The burgers, crispy roach bits and all, are served up and no one is the wiser. I vow never to eat burgers in this place again.

The next day we are making turkey-a-la-king, which means every left over from the week before can be smothered in a surreptitious sauce that envelopes everything, revealing nothing. The serving unit is a huge plastic drum that spits out individual servings with the opening and closing of a hinged jaw at the bottom. The drum has been used earlier that day to serve oatmeal and left unwashed, the oatmeal has crusted in hard ridges, dried into crevices of the wheel. I dutifully lift the wheel to take it to the sink to wash it out. The kitchen supervisor bellows at me, "Hey, whaddya think you're doing?" as he shoves the wheel out of my arms and back onto the counter. He flashes the menacing look at me again and I keep silent as the thick stream of turkey-a-la-king is loaded into the wheel where it can coax the stubborn oatmeal leftovers out of hiding, enfolding them in its creamy mass, promising them credibility once more as food fit for human consumption.

When the meal is over the kitchen supervisor dismisses everyone but me, leaving me behind to clean up all the pots alone. He pokes a stubby finger towards the wheel and growls, "Make sure that thing is clean," before leaving the kitchen to join the guards for a smoke. It's 11 p.m. before I finish my work in the kitchen and exhausted, I crawl onto my bunk, waiting for 5 a.m. to arrive and the breakfast ritual to begin the cycle again.

After that, I learn to keep my mouth shut and eat only the food the Oriental cooks prepare for themselves. They are happy to share, as agreeable as they are dangerous and I eat well. When the lock-down is over and it's time for me to leave, the kitchen supervisor nods a good-bye, a signal that in spite of my annoying penchant for sanitation, I'm a good worker.

MILLHAVEN A "TERRIBLE MESS"

It's "absolutely ridiculous" that three weeks of rioting at Millhaven prison have not been subdued, the Reform party's prison critic charged yesterday... do what "has to be done" to shut down the convict uprising.

"There is no call for this. The authorities have been rendered almost useless to deal with a violent gang that has literally gone out of control," Hanger charged after he toured the troubled maximum-security unit ranges....

Hanger's tour came the day after 27 Millhaven inmates ran amok in three separate ranges after they dug through concrete walls with broken desks and plumbing fixtures.

Hanger told *The Toronto Sun* the prison is in a "terrible mess."

"They complain about the food, but they've thrown the food all over the floor. It is a disgusting mess," Hanger said. "They're throwing feces and urine at the guards... they've done hundred's of thousands of dollars in damage...."

Eight inmates are confined in segregation amid fears of further trouble.

...Meanwhile, management says it's ready to negotiate inmate demands.

"We have to establish a contact with the inmates," acting warden Lou Kelly said yesterday. "Before we are able to return the institution to a normal routine, we are going to have to... make some sort of a compromise on each of the issues."

Prison officials have refused *Sun* requests to get in the prison and to meet inmates because the "situation is too volatile."

Inmates' demands include "yard privileges, full meals, open visits, access to the media and the resignation of warden Al Stevenson."

The Daily News
Friday February 7, 19___

Bill woke up angrier than usual. There was nothing special about the day, no special reason for hating the world and everything in it, but he had a real big hate on today, big enough to swallow this whole fucking prison and bury it and himself with it too. He felt nothing in his soul but a deep black hole fashioned by hate and cultivated by indifference. Bill was in a deadly frame of mind.

When they filed into the dining room Bill knew already that something was going to happen. He could smell it through the greasy, thick stink of the slop being thrust out on grimy metal trays through the service hole. Everything got served through the hole, which permitted the guards to stand back at least two feet from where the arms of any unruly prisoner could grab hold of them.

He scanned the room, taking in every subtlety with a glance. After fifteen years in this hole he knew every ridge in the steel-clad walls, every crack in the concrete floor as well as he knew his own hand, the hand that had pounded mercilessly through the jaws and eye-sockets of at least six guards in the past fifteen years. He'd spent at least three years in total in the hole, where you lie in the stench your own piss and shit for days at a time, but every minute of it worth it for the sheer pleasure of getting a little of your own back on them.

Bill observed the room thoroughly and imperceptibly, his eyes barely moving in their narrowed slits; he knew there was something, though he couldn't see it yet. But he detected a difference, a feeling, a pulse in the back of his throat told him there was some weakness today, some chink in the armour of corporal atonement. His eyes ticked off all the usual checks—there were no exterior doors in the dining area but heavy locks and chains secured the interior doors leading to the hallway that circled this hall and the kitchen behind it. All locks and chains were secured. Six vigilant guards stood in the bubble, heavily armed, no slumping shoulders, no idle hands, six pairs of eyes poised, strained, waiting and watching for any sign of trouble.

And then it jumped out at him. The door to the back kitchen, where guards and hired cooks prepared the foul crud that passed for food, had been left unlocked. A rare and singular opportunity, the kind that Bill and the others watched for, hoped for, every day. Jim had seen it too, and all it took was a bare, brief flash of an eye, not even a dropped eyelid, before at least a dozen of them knew, and saw, and understood that a momentous opportunity had just presented itself on this glorious day in hell.

It took Bill less than a second to leap from where he stood in the line-up straight to the kitchen door, flinging it open without a moment's hesitation. Six other inmates were close behind and within seconds they had three guards in numbing headlocks, too frozen with fear to struggle. The cook lay dead on the floor, blood pumping from his slit throat.

The inmates out in the dining area had reacted almost immediately, without hesitation, oblivious to the shots being fired through the open vents of the bubble. The frenzy of fists and bodies and blood-spilling continued in spite of the shots being fired by the guards. Within minutes all six guards had evacuated the bubble, sounding the alarm that rose in crescendo with the rising shouts and screams of the rioting inmates.

Tables, bolted solidly to the concrete floor, were suddenly ripped up and strewn about like toadstools, chairs were smashed against the walls, the floor, the men. The frenzied mass of muscle and bone and hair boiled up like a sea of vicious sharks seeking blood as every grudge that had been nursed through the past few months and years and lifetimes since the last such eruption, suddenly exploded with a second wind—the blessed chaos of anarchy.

Chaos. It was the next best thing to freedom.

DISRUPTIVE INMATES MOVED

Fourteen of the most disruptive inmates from the troubled maximum security unit at Millhaven penitentiary outside Kingston, Ont., were transferred yesterday to the more secure Special Handling Unit outside Montreal. The move came after the latest in a series of confrontations at the prison. Corrections Canada spokesperson ... said a group of prisoners began smashing their cells and setting fires Tuesday night. Inmates—who have been locked in their cells almost around the clock since a January 21 riot that left a prisoner dead—knocked down the walls between their cells. They didn't break out of their cells.

The Daily News
February 13, 19__

Chapter Twelve

February *20, 19__*

Dear W.,

I can't believe it's really going to happen—Outta here!! I'm writing this quickly while I wait to be called to the bus that's taking me and about eight other guys to our new "mother institutions." I don't know how many will be coming with me to Warkworth. I've heard lots of stories—good and bad—we'll see when I get there. But nothing could be worse than this place. Well, except where I was, that is, the good ol' stinkin' Don Jail.

Yeah, here I am DYING to get out of this hole, but just remembering for a moment the hell it was in that shithole makes this place look like a palace.

Sweetie, I know I've said it before but I'm going to say it again. Thank-you, from the bottom of my heart, for hanging in through all of this. You've been dragged through the most disgusting places you've ever been exposed to in your life and I wish to God you hadn't seen or experienced any of it. But I thank God every single day—every single minute—that you've had the guts to do it and see me through all of this. I really could not have made it this far in one piece, sanity relatively intact, without you.

It was so great to talk to you last night. I'll try to call the moment I get there, but I've heard horror stories of not getting a "pin number" for weeks after you arrive there. Without this precious "pin number" I can't make any phone calls, so this may be the last you hear from me for awhile. Don't worry about me, everything's going to be just fine, I know it. I mean, I really KNOW it, okay.

Gotta go, now, I'll put this in the mailbox as I leave. Kind of a parting ritual, eh? Right up your alley!

Remember, I love you!

Love, M.

FEBRUARY *23, 19___*

Dear M.,

Just got back from my meditation group. I think it's going to be really good for me. Tomorrow I'm going to really make an effort to wake up a bit early and do some meditation as soon as I'm awake, before I'm even out of bed. If I can get into the habit maybe eventually I'll do what you recommended—get up at 5 a.m. while the rest of the city is still asleep. What you said about not being bombarded by everyone's energy—that really makes sense.

I think that you have such an opportunity—maybe it's one of the only opportunities—in there, to get a clear mind—the ultimate Zen Buddhist state of "no mind." Because you have the time to do it. I know it must be terribly distracting with all those people and voices and nega-tivity but as one of the people in my group said, to achieve a practised meditative state you have to be able to do it in the marketplace, meaning noise and distractions should eventually be able to be ignored.

I thought also of what you wrote about "developing knowings," and not concentrating on breathing or anything, but just achieving perfect stillness. And that's what meditating is all about. It will go a long way to assist in your healing and overcoming the obstacles that in the past have brought you down.

I want to share with you one of the things I mentioned at the group tonight—we have a brief sharing at the end of the night. More and more lately, I feel as though my physicality and the rest of everything that surrounds me have less and less definition between them. Maybe it's only a split second, but I think I'm getting snatches of detachment, of being just soul and not body. Every once in a while I catch a fleeting image of my body being just atoms, points of light or energy that are not hard physical reality anymore, just part of all the other atoms and collections of energy that are perceived as real things—walls, floors, tables, trees, etc. Hope you get what I mean.

The other people at the group all talk about how few people are really into having a spiritual life, and how most of the world is still so caught up in the "reality" of human existence. Is that true? Why is it that I perceive that more and more people are discovering, or admitting to, their profound spiritual core? Is it just that I'm only being around people who have a spiritual life? I mean, at work no one would ever talk about this stuff so I guess it's true, probably most people are totally caught up in the material stuff.

But somehow I have the feeling that if it came down to a crunch, say we were all caught in a fire or a disaster of some sort, something life threatening, everyone would admit to believing in a lot more than they let on. I really don't believe that the whole world is going to hell. I think it's getting better just as much as it's getting worse, but even the fact that crime and terrorism and evil seem to have increased, is a sure sign that the good is also increasing, because that's the way it works, right?

The universe works in a constant balance, and as the good increases, so will the evil to try to counteract the good, but eventually one will win and the balance of one will start to decline as the other increases. Hopefully of course, it's the good that will increase as evil declines. Or maybe it will always be held in a perfect, equal balance, although we don't see it as equal because we don't see the whole picture and of course our perspective is so narrow. Maybe our perspective is totally out of whack anyway. I mean maybe the very tiniest bit of good or love that occurs far outweighs the greatest amount of evil that occurs, but we just don't know that.

One thing I do know is that love is all there is. Love is all that remains when life ends. Whatever we go on to in the next world or life or existence, the only thing that will last is the love we gave or received. Or does pain get carried on do you think? How else do you explain people who seem to have been born evil or hateful? Is it a carry-over from a previous life?

Did I tell you about that time when I was waiting to see you at the Don and I had the most amazing experience of being with you, where you were waiting on the other side, and I felt myself crawl into your lap and curl up there. And then I felt this incredible feeling of being outside of the human experience, outside of my hurt and my immediate reality. All I could feel was this incredible sense of love. It made me cry it was so powerful and I felt it so intensely.

All that will remain is the love. And I've remembered that moment ever since and when I get upset I try to draw on the strength of that moment. All we will remember is the love.

Love you, W.

I take four deep, full breaths but my heart is still pounding. I know exactly what I'll wear—I've known for weeks, I've set it out on the bed. My long grey skirt that swishes against my legs and feels so good, and the white cotton shirt, crisp, just dry-cleaned. Very casual, but neat and tidy. I feel terrified to go there, to see him. A joyful, bubbling, terrifying anxiety that almost makes me nauseous—no not almost, I *am* nauseous.

It's been a year since we touched—God, I have to stop crying, how can I put on make-up like this. And I *will* wear make-up. I want to look beautiful, to look perfect for him.

Yes, I'm dressing up to go to prison, so who cares? Who has to know that I feel this way inside, that I'm terrified and too excited and can barely drink my coffee or hold my mascara brush without my hand shaking and smearing it all over. Twice I've had to wash away the smears and start over.

Finally, I'm ready. I smooth my hand over the long grey skirt and swish it out to one side to make myself feel it, that sense of here I am, I'm going to be seen and heard and I'm not scared of anything, I can do this. It's very convincing to watch, even I'm impressed and I know it's an act. I check for the hundredth time that my passport and driver's license are both in my purse.

I read the directions again, and take another look at the map, though it's too small a place to show anything more than a tiny dot with the place name "Warkworth." I look at the clock again, and it's only 5:30 a.m. Even if it takes me the full three hours they said it would, I'll still be there early. Good. Early is good, even if it means waiting longer. What if it's like the Don or worse, like Millhaven and I don't even get the visit cause there's ten people ahead of me?

In the car I keep pushing buttons to change radio stations. I shove in a cassette and pop it out again. Nothing sounds right, I'll just have silence. But the silence reminds me of my lurching stomach, my pounding heart, the tears that I'm just barely holding back.

Finally I'm at the turn-off. I drive up Hwy 45, it seems far, *what if I've passed it?!* Finally I see a sign, I almost miss the turn, my tires crunch hard on the gravel as I wheel left. I drive further on into town, looking for the road that the female guard had named when I had phoned for directions. It's not here, where's the water tower she mentioned?

The panic is beginning to get the better of me now. I drive on through past the cluster of stores and businesses, I've driven straight through town, now and still no road she had named. I stomp hard on the brakes, almost crying but biting back as hard as I can on the fear. "What's the fear?" I ask myself. Fear of not getting in to see him? Fear of having to wait days, or hours longer? Fear that I might do something absolutely crazy if they don't let me in, if I haven't quite dotted the "I's" right, or crossed the "T's" just so, that they'll have an excuse to turn me away?

I'm almost sobbing now, but I have to pull myself together enough to go into someplace and ask where it is. It's still early for a sleepy little town, nothing looks open. A farm supply place, seeds and stuff, they're open.

I get out of the car, holding my breath, pushing it out again, watching it fade and disappear into the coolness of the early day. How do I ask, what do I say? What if they snap shut suddenly when I ask the question, what if they hate us all, the scum in the prison and their wives and children and sisters and lovers… "Excuse me, can you tell me how I get to Warkworth Institution, please?"

It's only a blink of an eye, barely any hesitation, but I catch it, waiting for it, expecting it, like a bird prying its breakfast out of the dewy grass. I know it's buried there. The thought flashes that maybe I want it, the look, the judgement, maybe it has come to define me in some way. *Yes, I am a wife, a lover, of one of them.* She directs me back out along the road I came, I should have turned right where I turned left, it's further up the road. I feel her eyes on me as I thank her and leave. There is no smile returning mine.

Back in the car, I can't hold the tears back any longer, my careful makeup job is ruined by the jets pouring out of my eyes; I can barely see the road. Thank God it's early and there are no other cars, I'm driving like a maniac on this gravel road, who cares about the stones denting the car, *I can't be late, I have to get there!!!*

It's only ten minutes up the road, and I drive straight through at the intersection where I zigged when I should have zagged. I laugh through tears at the memory of the joke, though I don't even remember the joke any more. I laugh again when I see the water tower, looming huge up ahead, how on earth I could have missed it is a mystery, God what an idiot I am sometimes. Nervous laughter, the laughter of relief, tears still fresh in my eyes. I'm almost there, and it's only just past 9 a.m. I regret now having stopped for that coffee, thinking I had time to kill. It's going to be fine, I tell myself. Everything's going to be fine and I've finished with counting down the weeks and days and hours. Now it's only minutes. It's only a matter of *minutes* 'til I can touch him, 'til he can hold me.

I get there and the angels have smoothed the way for me. There's hardly any line-up, I sign in and terrified, I do exactly as instructed, removing all my jewellery except my grandmother's bracelets that don't come off and what if they tell me I have to remove them to go in. Well, if they do, I'll get them off somehow; I breathe down the panic, they pass the wand over me and blessing of all blessings, the guard is the same woman I spoke to on the phone and she remembers my name.

She lets me through with a smile and I think in dismay of how different all of this is from the wickedness of the Don Jail and Millhaven visiting ordeal. There are two more doors to get buzzed through, there's a small group of us, mostly women, one man and a boy child. Books are not allowed in the boy is told, but this guard is a kind one, one of the few I will later learn, and she allows the boy to bring his book with him.

I'm pacing waiting for the door to open. I speak to another wife, I'm babbling *"more than a year since we've touched..."* She's been there, she knows, but she's not in the mood for my spluttering. I cringe with embarrassment when I later recall this moment. The second and final door is buzzed open, I go through it and straight to the guard's window as instructed and they tell me to just go and sit somewhere and wait. I look then at the visiting room, and shock registers at how nice it is—huge and bright with lots of windows and a courtyard and a play area for the kids. My God, is this real? How can it be so *different?*

It seems like hours more to wait for him to come through the door from his side, and I can't sit down and wait, I prowl in front of the door like a lioness, watching my feet, counting my paces. The door opens and I snap my head up to look but it's not him. It opens again, same thing, and now the panic is rising again, the tears have started, God I can't stand it, where is he, *where is he?!*

When the door finally opens on him, I am shaking, tears pouring down my face. I can't move towards him at first, can't move at all, it's all so much to hold in I can't do it, I'm hugging myself so hard I later find bruises on both arms. He reaches for me and I grab hold of his neck and bury my face deep down into the well of his collarbone. I'm sobbing, "Don't let go. Please don't let go." I can barely get the words out, they aren't meant to be words at all, they are a mantra that I repeat just to keep from melting away into tears. He holds me hard against him, stroking my hair with one hand, and softly in my ear I almost hear him saying, "Shush, it's okay now, I'm not going to let go."

It's ten minutes at least like that before we move, we're almost blocking the doorway for the others as they come out for their visit, but like time, judgement is standing still and the sheer emotion of this moment can't help but be felt by the others so that they step around us in respect. I finally stop crying long enough to pull my face back to look up into his and the deep blueness is still there, it's still him, he is still the man I know. He presses his cheek hard against mine, I know he's choking back a sob himself, though no one else would know it.

He keeps holding me hard around the waist as he walks me over to a table and we sit together, still clutching each other like life preservers. I insist on sitting on his knee, the way that Joanne Woodward sat on Paul Newman's knee in that movie where they were married, but she had gotten old and they had fallen out of passion. But still, she was his wife and they loved each other in that way you do after so long and he could comfort her that way—it was ownership of some kind, ownership of the bond.

The guard in the bubble calls his name out over the speaker and he has to go up to the bubble where the guard advises him that I'm not allowed to sit on his knee. The angels have arranged once again, for a kind guard to tell us this, and I never see this one again on any other visits. So we sit face to face, but our knees are not allowed to touch. We lean together in a tight embrace and I cry some more into his neck, smelling deep into his skin, remembering the smell of him and crying more when I do.

Half an hour later we're laughing, both incredulous at the wonder of this love, so powerful that it has simply melted away the rocks and stones of the past year of separation. "It's over," we both tell each other, awestruck at the fact that the being apart for so long could disappear so suddenly, disappear out of existence altogether. "It's gone, isn't it, we'll never have to be apart again," I whisper. I'm smiling now, though the sobs are still intermittent. He strokes my face again, my hair and his voice is the sweetest, most melodic sound I have ever heard. "Sweet thing, I *promise* you we will never be apart again."

And the promise is more than a vow, it is a prediction, a truth come into being. It is, in it's moment of being spoken, creating its own fulfilment.

FEBRUARY 28, 19__

Hey Sweetie,

I'm counting the hours to see you again! Unfortunately, I got my long-distance bill and the bad news is, it's no cheaper than it was from Kingston. So we have to cut back a bit until I can get it down to something I can handle—it's over $400.00 now! I got nowhere trying to talk to someone in customer service at Bell. They blame the policies of Correctional Services, Correctional Services blames Bell. Big surprise. Anyway, it's only a week between visits! A MIRACLE!

I don't know whether I can keep up both days every weekend though, these last two weekends have left me utterly, completely exhausted.

I guess these letters are going to get sparse now, but you know we really should try to keep it up. That's one really amazingly good thing that has come out of this separation. We wrote out everything we were feeling, and YOU even really told me what you were feeling and thinking. I so enjoyed your letters, please write me some more!

I'm putting all your stuff together and hoping they'll let me drop it off on a visit, 'cause a courier is going to cost a fortune. Are you sure that I have to courier everything, 'cause I heard the guards in the

"Search" area telling someone that you can "move in the contents of your whole house as long as it's within the 30-day period" and then after that you can't even send a birthday or Christmas present. I mean, how would people send in furniture and other big stuff, which I'm sure lots of people bring in, and T.V.s, etc.? There must be some other way of sending stuff.

I've looked through your clothes and I'll have to buy some socks and maybe another sweater? Let me know what you need. There's quite a bit of your clothes I can send—I mean, they fall within the regulations of colour, etc. that are on the form you gave me.

I guess I'm writing this now and by the time you read it we'll already have talked about it all, but still, I like writing to you. It helps to get all these things out on paper and not have to wait to tell you things.

I've done some more thinking (surprise, surprise!) and I came to another realization about why and how I went through this whole thing alone. Even after I discovered "JustUs," it wasn't enough because by that time it was too late to be able to rely on a support group to "get me through" the worst time—too much had already happened.

But anyway, I really understand something about it all now. I was so angry and felt so deserted by God for having to go through this alone. I realize now that my strength was in my total aloneness. That's how I got through it. Being alone was the only way I could have done this. My strength came from knowing that no one was going to be able to advise me on what I should do, no one would be there to hold me when the going got rough and so I had to depend on myself or perish.

And now look at us. Look at what we've come through. A few days and nights of depression, even despair, but look, we're still in the game. We're still together, stronger and more determined than ever that we won't let time or space or ANYTHING tear us apart.

I went to see a movie tonight—I love going to movies alone! It wasn't romantic, or anything, but I couldn't help remembering that night when you came back from out West and you took me out for dinner and a movie. Our first "date," after all that time apart, remember? It was that night that I realized and understood why I loved you so much and why it had to be you.

It's simple—you want me. You've always wanted me. And that's the only thing I've ever wanted. To feel wanted. I've heard all my girlfriends say the same thing, relationships don't work because the men just don't want them enough (I mean besides the sex).

But it seems like there's always one woman that a man really, REALLY wants and he'll do anything to be with her. I am that one woman for you. And now, realizing that, I feel like everything will be alright, of course it will. I am with THE man who wants me. I am THE WOMAN that you want. And that's worth waiting a lifetime for.

I love you, W.

From W's Journal

MARCH 23, 19__

I hate Hollywood. It glamorizes tragedy until it's unrecognizable. Life according to Hollywood is a series of great and glorious romantic moments, all sewn together perfectly in an exquisite tapestry of the most delicate detail. The truth of life is that it is a changeable cloak, woven yes, but not always of silk, mostly of burlap, rough against the skin.

Character is the warp and experience is the weft. The shuttle is moved along by events, people and circumstances, bringing the threads together in patterns; many are exquisite, some plain and others very complex, but to the creator I suppose they all are beautiful. If only we could view it all from the creator's lofty seat. If only we could view it as simply a mantle we wear for the moment, not permanent, not forever, not so all important as it seems. A cloak of many colours. A cloak that can be exchanged for another. A lesser one, a greater one, this one has more orange in it, that one has more blue; this one feels warm and fits so well, that other was always too tight around the neck.

I hate Hollywood. Grief is made so romantic and beautiful and graceful and in the movie the heroine is someone you long to be, you relate to her, you feel her tragedy, the pureness of her struggle against death and loneliness and despair. The strains of the weeping violins seep warmly through your soul like a scented oil, the pungence of its aroma soothing and stirring and sweet. And suddenly one morning the heroine, her hair brilliant and perfectly backlit, awakes from her grieving and is briskly alive again, renewed, rebirthed. Hallelujah! as the strings fade away and the horns blow ever so softly and the new hero in her life leans into a halo of sunlit trees to kiss the heroine's hand.

The heroine's dead, doesn't anybody get that yet? She died along with Cinderella and Sleeping Beauty and even Prince Charming—he kicked it long ago. They're all dead, so why do we go on singing the Hollywood dream?

I guess it all sounds bitter of me. But truly, why do we get off so much on glorifying tragedy. Tragic love, it's been the subject of myths and stories and legends forever, it's the stuff we crave, we love to make it so large that it blots out all the mundaneness of real life; the plodding of real love and the greyness of romance. We weep at its beauty, the singular simplicity of its straining note, it's striving chord. We reach for it and gasp when we open our hands to find we have seized again only the ordinary, the simple and sadly, shamefully, we sink down to reality again.

Life is so hard, and sometimes it does feel beautiful but it shames reality to glorify it that way. Real love and passion are so minimized when they are mimicked in front of the camera. The perfect-making of romance steals its flavour like an over-salted dish.

When this is all over I won't remember why I cried so much and why it hurt so much. I won't fucking remember.

I must remember WHY. But there is no why. It's just there like a great, slimy, sticky ball of goo in your throat. It sticks there and keeps coming up but it never comes out and you just cry and cry.

Everything I do in my life right now is merely a distraction, a different kind of movie, played on a screen that I sit in front of to pass the time. A lengthy litany of distracting words and actions and thoughts, carelessly tossed out onto the stage of my mind, for the sole purpose of distraction, keeping my mind busy while my heart retreats.

But *this* movie, while punctuated often by grief and humour, courage and fear, is certainly not made in HOLLYWOOD. It has no orchestra, no lighting, no sound. It has no one standing by to feed me my lines or change the script if the need should arise. I can't change the direction of the plot simply by pencilling notes in the margin, or erasing events that don't carry over well onto the big screen.

I read that the ancient Greeks believed that humans were the entertainment of the gods, that watching our little lives, our loves and our betrayals, this was their sport. We were their Hollywood. What a dull entertainment we would seem, next to the movie-making perfection of today. Where was the subdued lighting, the dubbed-in singing of the actress who can't actually carry a note, where was the music and staging and glory?

I guess those gods were satisfied with the dullness of John and Jane struggling every step of the way through their lessons, straining to simply be with it all and not lose their minds, their hearts. Passing and failing the innumerable tests of courage and cunning and strength never knowing what outcome a choice will create. I guess that was true suspense, the not knowing how it will all turn out.

Well, I guess the gods would be pleased with us in this turn of events. They don't know how it will all turn out. We don't know how it will all turn out. But whether its the gods or God, I know they are in it. I know God is in it, I know that God sees. I know God is watching and waiting for us to come to our senses, to learn what we know, to remember all that was given to us in the very beginning. We are coming to know all these truths again.

We are carrying ourselves through the jungles of unknowing and bumping along the road of indecision, assailed by fear and greed and the menacing shadow of despair. We are emptied by lovelessness, stopped in our tracks, staring blankly at walls that suddenly appear along the way, not knowing a way through or around but some of us get there somehow. In the midst of our despair, we find the hope to continue the journey.

Hope, in fact, seems to arrive at precisely the moment that we exhaust despair.

Chapter Thirteen

April 15, 19___
Dear M.,

I'm coming to see you tomorrow, but I want to write down a few thoughts anyway, and I'll drop this letter in the mailbox they have in the "search" area outside the visit room.

God, that whole "search" scene is something wild, I really have to write it down sometime so that I'll always remember—I mean, I owe it to all of them who are still going through it long after we've left and continued with our lives; I owe it to all those wives and mothers and brothers and sons to remember.

So often I think to myself that when this is all over I'm going to walk away and leave the memories behind and never return to them again. But lately I've been feeling that it would be some kind of betrayal. This is my experience, all these moments of frustration, anxiety, joy (at seeing you!), fear, and on and on, the whole drama. There is a sense of "letting go" in the idea of walking away and forgetting everything as though it never happened, which is what part of me really wants to do. But more and more I'm feeling as though doing that would be betraying myself somehow and would also be showing disrespect for the reality of all those who are still in it.

Without being corny, it's true that we are all in it together and only those of us who live it know what this is really like. Hey—it just occurs to me that all these thoughts I'm having reflect the whole "All is One" philosophy and taken on a larger scale, the whole of human experience is to be shared in this way. We are not simply individuals experiencing life subjectively; as parts of one whole creation, a single divine energetic SYSTEM, we are united by our experience, we all experience it even though so many of us are not aware that this is so.

I guess my acknowledgement that I continue to experience this with the others even after I have left the visit room forever, left the humiliation and loneliness and longing behind, this is real awareness of my humanity, of what it means to be human. It is all one, we are all part of one another's experiences and we laugh, cry, weep and die together whether we know it or not.

God, all this philosophy makes my head hurt. I think writing these thoughts to you is easier than trying to talk about it there in the visit room. They seem like such private thoughts and so large that they need room to be spoken, to be spread out and looked at and pondered and all of this requires a privacy that we just don't have yet.

Oh, something I have to tell you. I forgot I had your jean jacket and I just remembered it today. I went with my friend S. when she did her laundry tonight and she had washed her boyfriend's jean jacket and she wore it home. It made me really sad until I remembered that I have MY sweetheart's jean jacket TOO, and so I ran home and got it out of the closet and I'm wearing it right now. And I'm going to wear it whenever I feel like I need something extra to feel connected to you. So silly, isn't it, but a jean jacket—it's like a ring or something, it's that special thing between lovers and when you "belong" to someone it's just one of those things. A little thing of belonging to be able to wear your lover's jean jacket.

Yeah, yeah, I know, I'm getting really schlocky in my old age. Can't wait to see you tomorrow. Now I get to go to sleep and when I wake up (at 6 a.m.!) it'll be time to come and see you—I love that, the fact that I can go to bed and the waiting time disappears.

Love you, W.

From W's Journal
May 2, 19__

I'm so tired of feeling shame. Of hiding myself for fear of exposing some weakness, some shameful behaviour. I'm sick to DEATH of inhibition, of guilt, of telling myself—No! you can't have this or you must not do that or if you have it or do it you must punish yourself with guilt and regret and shameful remorse.

I want to have FUN! But I need to feel safe. I have no protector, no lover standing behind me, beside me, living to defend me and love me into all that I am, *"because of,"* not just "in spite of."

This feeling of being SICK of feeling so constrained, this will give way, will open that hidden door to freedom, where I no longer GIVE A SHIT WHAT people think of me or say of me.

I YAM WHO I YAM!!!!

And for love or hate of me, it makes no difference, I am still me.

June 22, 19__
Dear W.,

Just got your letter—the one with the stamps and stuff. Thanks, it will save me a few bucks on canteen day.

I'm starting to get settled into my new cell and I get along pretty well with my new cellmate. He is a lot like me except that he doesn't have a spiritual bone in his body. That surprises me considering he is half Native. He respects my space though, so I'm very lucky.

Things are pretty routine here in "Reception" and time is starting to slow down a bit. Yeah, I know, we thought that Millhaven was "Reception," but each time they move you to another institution you're in reception again, and the wait begins AGAIN. Except now that I'm here to actually do my time, the wait shouldn't be as long. It's hard to know, though since policy and reality don't seem to collide much in here.

22-hour lock-up offers little as far as breaking up the day goes, but the weekends are okay. We get three hours Yard in the morning and then the regular 8:30 to 10:30 at night. Lots of stuff to do in the Yard, come summertime—half-mile track, mini-putt, volleyball, tennis, horse-shoes, weights, basketball. If you want to go into the gym, you can play floor hockey, pool and other stuff.

I'm really struggling with this letter to B., can't seem to find the right words. What do I say to an ex-wife who hated me before all of this, and now has the justification to hate me and condemn me even more? This only serves to give her opinion of me some teeth.

I think I'll just write it and send it however it comes out, because I want so much to have some contact with the girls. I'm feeling like there is more I should be doing or things are just not going fast enough. As far as the girls are concerned, I guess I should force the issue and insist that she let me write to them and make sure they get the letters. But on a day to day basis, there's not much I can do from in here.

This place is one big warehouse. Nothing is really going to happen until I get my programmes completed, and the waiting list is so long that I'm at about number 260 something, but I'm not even officially "on the list" until I'm out of "Reception." My cellmate's been here four months and he's still in the 200s so I don't expect things to move very quickly—or efficiently.

My god, you would just not BELIEVE the waste and misuse that is rampant within this system. I'm sure there's no one to tell that could have any effect on any of it, but it utterly astounds me to see how little these guards and "classification officers" work, how much waste there is, and how NO ONE seems to have to answer for any of it. They spend their days mostly on smoke breaks and drinking coffee. If you ask for any-thing, they look at you like you're some kind of cockroach or something.

Well patience is certainly a virtue and it's one I will have to learn in here. Remember how nuts I always used to go when I would have to wait for ANYTHING?! There's nothing to do here, BUT wait. Even when there are so many things you should be doing, and could be doing to help yourself, there is no way to do them. This has got to be the best school for learning patience. It's just like you talk about, I'm here to get the lessons in life that I've fought hardest against. Those are the lessons I need in order to progress spiritually and I guess patience is going to be the basic ingredient.

Well, I'm gonna go now, I'll see you again in the visit room before you even get this letter. Isn't it great!! But the week in between feels so long. And the phone calls just aren't long enough, especially when I know how much they're costing you and I don't want to keep you on there too long. But every time I hang up I feel like I had other stuff to say.

Miss you!

M.

JULY 25, 19___

Dear M.,

Just waiting for you to call. It's been a pretty frustrating week so far. No car and everything. I miss you so much. I just hope my car is ready by the weekend. Please understand that if I don't have a car this weekend, I'll miss our visit. I'm just not up to the hassle of a bus trip right now.

I finally tried to put up my kitchen shelf—the eating counter that's been sitting in its wrapping for more than a year. What an exercise in frustration. I just can't do this stuff, and even if I can, I hate it. I hate doing "man things" and it makes me miss you even more, and on a practical note, rather than emotional. Except it becomes emotional cause it just reminds me how much I HATE being on my own all the time and how long the road stretches ahead alone. God I can't wait for this to be over.

But once we get our weekends and we can finally be alone together, at least I won't feel as bad, 'though my shelf may still not be up until you get home.

I've written to the Warden (again!—letter three and counting) to find out WHEN we are getting our "trailer" visits.

Anyway I'm pissed off and frustrated and I wish you were here. (Not necessarily in that order).

Love you and hope to see you before you get this letter.

W.

August 7, 19__
Dear Sweetie,

Well, you're probably in the plane by now, flying far away from me. I'm really going to miss you but I'm so glad you're getting away from everything for awhile. You really need this break.

So, I got called to the "Hospital" today. The doctor wanted to examine the X-rays of my back. Then he realized that he hadn't taken them yet and sent me back to my cell. What a joke. This, after how many months of requests? I had put in a request last month to get my legal and medical records sent to me and I was just called in to sign a consent form. The request hasn't even been processed yet! I think I might have told you about this on our visit.

I'm still struggling with this letter to B. I never got a response to the first one and I don't know if she's just not accepting my collect calls or if she's just not home all the time but all I ever get when I try to call is "the charges have been refused," which could mean the machine picked up. It's impossibly frustrating to try to call someone collect when you don't know if they'll even take the call.

I can't seem to find the opening words for this letter. I know it really doesn't matter what she thinks of me. I don't feel the need to justify or explain my actions to her in any way but at the same time I don't want to give her any justification for keeping the girls away from me. Or maybe it does matter what she thinks, not from my point of view, but perhaps there's another side to the coin.

I mean, if you separate all the personality conflicts between us, and all the resentments from previous events, do I owe her some explanation for my actions? Not from me to her but from an irresponsible father to a single mother trying to raise three children on her own. Do I owe her some sort of an explanation or even an apology for having done something that has probably impacted on her life, and certainly on the life of our children? Is my trying to just pacify her a cop-out in some way, avoiding the truth of my responsibility, manipulating to avoid the guilt of what I've done to my children?

Please share your thoughts on this with me, W. I feel like this thing is holding me back now. It's time to deal with this but I want to make sure I deal with it appropriately. When I get out of here I want to know that I didn't leave any loose ends as far as how I feel about myself. When I get out, I don't want the burden of suppressed feelings holding me back. Holding us back.

AUGUST 15, 19__

Got your postcards today and I miss you more than words can say. But at least I know you're safe and sound and that puts my mind at ease. I've been worrying non-stop about you and now I wish I had insisted on you going with someone instead of going on your own. I don't know what I would ever do if I lost you, now.

Enough of those thoughts. Only one more week 'til I see you!

My favourite show is on in about 45 minutes and even though it's my cellmate's T.V. he always lets me watch it—"T.L.C.—The Miracle Planet."

AUGUST 16, 19__

Good morning Sweetie. Looks like its going to be a beautiful day. There is a huge outdoor activities area here—way bigger than any of the Yards in the other jails I've been in so far. And there's a smaller yard too, where it's quiet, some trees with benches under them. I'm going to sit out there today and try to get caught up on some of these letters I need to write.

Just came back inside. Too busy out there. You won't believe it— found a "bleach kit" on my bed. The guards handed them out for cleaning needles, what a joke. I guess it's a good thing. I mean there's no way to eradicate the drug problem here, it's absolutely endemic in the system. Hell, the guards at Millhaven and the Don Jail DEPEND on the drug trade.

I may be in line for a great job. Cleaning the trailers (the "private family visiting" units—you know, the "love shacks"—where we're gonna be soon!!) My cell partner does it now and he'll be getting moved soon. He only works one day a week and gets to spend one night in one of the trailers. (Great for me, cause I would actually get a whole night alone without all the thunderous noise that always goes on here, 24 hours a day.) Anyway, he said he's recommended me for the job when he leaves, but we don't know if there's already somebody else in line for it.

Well, I should go now and try to get some of those other letters written. It's pretty tough when you're writing real letters, I mean when you have something significant and deep that you need to express. Not just the usual, Hi how are you, blah blah blah bullshit. I mean, I find it physically exhausting. What makes it worse is not knowing whether the person you're writing to is going to understand what you're trying to tell them.

I've been thinking a lot about my sister Carol since I got her (one and only) letter. Crazy as it may seem to you, because I know how you feel about what she's done (or not done), I think I owe her an apology and some kind of explanation. I mean, I've done something here that will have a huge effect on her children's lives not only from the perspective of me being their uncle but having permitted their father to get involved. Yeah, he chose it and he's a grown man and everything but he never would have, never could have come up with anything like this on his own.

I started something that has put an end to the relationship between her two sons and their father. It's not up to me to judge whether the relationship was healthy or not for the boys. I think that saying, "Well, D. was an asshole anyway and the boys are better off without him," would be just another cop-out on my part. The bottom line is, I very well know that those boys love their Dad and he loves them, even if he's very stupid about how he shows it.

And even though D. made his own decisions, it was me who presented him with the opportunity. I mean I didn't want him to get involved, God knows I knew he was a liability from the get-go (as he proved to be). But hell, I showed a weak-minded idiot a chance to get his hands on a whole lot of money and what else was he going to do but beg to be let in on it? Given the fact that he trusted me and looked up to me, I could even say that in some small way, I set him up, even though not intentionally.

Now his kids may never see him again. Someday, I'm going to have to sit those boys down and tell them that this wasn't their father's fault, that I led him into this whole thing. And their mother just wasn't emotionally equipped to deal with it any better than she did, so she just reacted and took them away from their father for good. And for all of that, I am truly sorry.

I also believe that this is some of the reason that Carol has reacted in the way that she has; "deserted" me, as you see it. She just doesn't have the emotional strength to deal with it in any other way. But hell, can you really blame her? I mean look at her life.

She never had the chance to develop ANY kind of life skills. At a time when her life was finally seeming to get on track, i.e. she for once had created the hope of a normal life—a job with a possible future, a steady, dependable guy that she could build a relationship with who could provide her with a home and opportunities she could only dream of before—why wouldn't she have reacted the way she did? Protect it at any cost, even if it meant turning her back on me (and you). She had to pour her energy into her own life and who can blame her for that?

I know one thing for sure. If she had dealt with it differently, i.e. if she had stood by me through this and as a result had messed up her job or her relationship because she couldn't handle it, I'd have a lot more to feel guilty about. At least I haven't caused her to ruin her life.

Anyway, Sweetie, I want to get started on writing these other letters, so I'll say good-bye for now.

Love, M.

Chapter Fourteen

In the depth of the dark night of the soul, the veil between
transformation and despair, or madness, has waned so thin it
becomes transparent.

So that, standing behind it in the throes of our suffering, we open
wide our eyes and see it all before us, the pit... and the rope.

We can grasp the rope and fight our way up it into the light
Or we can jump, too terrified to even reach for it, our one faint hope.
Some will reach for it, some will climb.
They will walk out onto solid ground and daylight.
Others, too, will reach for it, but weakened by their sojourn in
the darkness... their strength gives out.

They shall find their final peace in the abyss.
And soft! the Stillness and the Night
Embrace the dying of the Light

◈

JAIL SUICIDES IMPOSSIBLE TO PREVENT, INQUEST TOLD

Nothing can prevent a prisoner determined to commit suicide from taking his life, a correctional service supervisor with more than two decades in Metro jails has told an inquest.

Roberto Carlos Pacheco, 23, was so determined to die he knotted one end of a sheet to the bottom of the upper bunk in his Toronto (Don) Jail cell and made a slip knot with the other, the inquest heard yesterday....

Although the death came in the middle of an Ontario Public Service Employees Union strike, staffing on the shift was unaffected and there were the usual number of cell checks, the inquest has been told."

The Daily News
September 4, 19__

INTERVIEW WITH AN INMATE

September 19___

Interviewer: You were in the Don Jail during the strike by the Ontario Public Service Employees—Correctional Services guards being among them. How long did the strike last?

Inmate: About a month, more or less.

Interviewer: Did you find that the strike affected you personally?

Inmate: Absolutely.

Interviewer: In what ways?

Inmate: Well, restrictions of not only privileges but basic human rights.

Interviewer: Such as?

Inmate: Clean, dry clothes. Access to showers. Personal safety. Food.

Interviewer: Are you saying they didn't feed you?

Inmate: Meals were cut back to sometimes one or two a day because they were down to skeleton staff and so they didn't have enough guards to deliver meals. When they did come, *always* they were ice cold—we got one warm meal during the entire strike. Typically, under "normal" conditions at the Don, the food is something you would have to think twice about before you fed it to your dog, so these meals, when they're ice cold—well, you can imagine. But if you're hungry enough—you eat. Plus, you can't afford to let yourself get weak. You have to keep up your strength.

Interviewer: It was reported that inmates were being served McDonald's during the strike.

Inmate: During the final days of the strike, they did get food brought in twice a day. I think it was McDonald's or something—whatever was cheapest. But it was cold by the time you got it.

Interviewer: You say they were down to skeleton staff. Did that affect cell checks at all?

Inmate: They just didn't happen. Cell checks never really do happen in the Don though, it's not like they actually *do* cell checks at night. Though, I'm sure there are areas where they have to swipe a card or something to prove they've done their rounds. But it's not as though they actually look into the cells.

Interviewer: There was an inmate who committed suicide during that strike. Were you aware of the incident?

Inmate: I lived three cells away from him.

Interviewer: What do you remember about him?

Inmate: He was the kind of kid—you could tell—was really fucked up in his head but was trying to maintain his sense of self-respect by putting on a big show of bravado. I mean, his case was really high profile—and that gave him some twisted sort of celebrity. So he played it up. But you could tell that he knew he was in deep trouble.

Interviewer: You mean from the charges he was facing?

Inmate: I'm not at liberty to discuss anybody's charges, but it was common knowledge that this kid was charged jointly with police officers in an armoured car robbery and that there is a lot of unrecovered money.

Interviewer: So, are you saying the "kid" was in danger? Perhaps from his co-accused, or maybe from others who wanted to get their hands on this money?

Inmate: I'm saying, the kid was in a lot more trouble than most people realized. He was in trouble in or out of jail. And he knew that.

Interviewer: Did you ever speak to him?

Inmate: Yes.

Interviewer: And did he seem suicidal, did you think?

Inmate: He was frantic. He was always frantically trying to get a phone and he couldn't even dial the numbers himself—he had to get someone else to dial the numbers for him. And this constant state of panic was visible to *everyone* including the guards. He was using the word "suicide," loosely, for days before it happened.

Interviewer: Loosely, in what way?

Inmate: I'm not naming names, but I know that he asked more than one person if they'd help him. And I was told, directly, by one of those people that he had tipped off a guard.

Interviewer: So you're saying that at least one guard may have had knowledge of his suicidal state of mind, but nothing was done about it?

Inmate: I'm saying that *nobody* could have missed the fact that this kid was suicidal. In spite of skeleton staff, he should have received closer attention, which he obviously needed. Had he gotten closer supervision, his state of mind would have been obvious to the authorities.

I mean, the fact is, during that strike, with the conditions we were living in—no clean or dry sheets or clothing, showers every few days, the food—I mean, almost everyone was feeling suicidal, including myself. And the staff were using that, trying to incite riots in order to prove their own point, in order to force conciliation for their demands and they used us to try to do this. It was clear to all of us, and the funny thing about it is, that knowing we were being used and knowing they were trying to incite us to riot, it was much quieter, I was told, than normal, as far as violence amongst the population goes.

Interviewer: Do you think Pacheco's death was suicide?

Inmate: I think he was definitely in the frame of mind to kill himself. I mean, nobody was surprised when we heard about it. But given the way that they found him, it was a pretty strange suicide. I mean, some people thought he may have had some help.

...The armed robbery suspect—dead for between four and six hours before guards found him—hung another sheet so that the patrolling guards view into the bunk was obscured.

His cellmate found him on the morning of March 17, 19__, face down with his legs on the bunk. His body was suspended and held at an angle by the ligature.

The inquest has been told the correctional officer on duty looked into Pacheco's cell between 12 and 18 times during his shift. But Pacheco was partially obscured by a sheet and the night light in the cell was blocked by newspaper glued on with toothpaste.

It was not until his cellmate woke at about 8 a.m. and raised the alarm that Pacheco's death was discovered.

And nothing would have stopped him from killing himself ... Smith, an operations manager at the jail, testified yesterday.

"If I sat outside Mr. Pacheco's [cell] door 24 hours a day ... if Mr. Pacheco was going to commit suicide, he would have done it," Smith said.

...Smith went on to say that in the face of this, recommendations on how to prevent suicide were pointless."

The Daily News
September 4, 19__

STUDY FOUND PRISON GUARDS "INSENSITIVE"

A study finding that most correctional guards have a bad attitude toward offenders says that is something that must change if the rising rate of suicides in Canada's prisons is to be controlled.

A 1994 federal study says 80 percent of prison guards hold "punitive attitudes toward offenders," which could hurt efforts to prevent prison suicides.

"Staff who are burned out and have poor control over their biases and prejudices can trigger suicides," the study found.

...People who work behind prison walls say there is a good reason guards are insensitive.

"Sometimes [guards] look at the inmates as something less than
human beings," says one former prison counsellor... It's a defence
mechanism. The guards say they don't want to be friendly with
someone they might have to shoot...."

The Daily News
July 31, 19__

"So, what exactly is the feeling, how would you describe what you're
feeling about this?" his voice is soft and soothing, encouraging, safe.

"It's... it's like being suffocated. Stuffed into a bottle with a cork on it and
ready to just explode out of it because if I don't get myself out of this bottle,
I'll die." My hand goes instinctively to my throat, it gets harder and harder to
push my breath out of my body.

"Now, this is more than once I'm hearing you talk about dying." He is
matter of fact. And he remembers every word of every session.

"Well, I'm ... I think, I mean, I thought I was past all of that—I hadn't had
these thoughts in so long I thought I had beaten it, but... this week, it's been
so bad, I... I thought about suicide again." I stare down at the carpet, embarrassed to look up at him, but I feel his eyes fixed on me, never wavering. If I
look up I know they will be soft and brown, no judgement, no exasperation,
just simple human kindness and the desire to awaken understanding.

"So... you feel like if you don't act, if you don't do *something*, though you
don't know what that something is, you will die, or you will kill yourself.
Now, what that makes me think, is, what is it in you that wants to die? In
other words, what part of you is ready to die?"

"Um... oh... my God. Oh my God, you're right. I never saw it that way
before." I take my hand away from my throat. "It's only a symbol. I don't really
want to kill myself, just this part of me. Yes, it's just this part of me—but...
what part is that?" I'm not afraid now to look up and see the eyes, intent,
meeting mine steadily.

"Hmm, yeah, well, that's the question to ask yourself, isn't it." He laughs,
and then gestures me to invite myself inside and ask it.

Twenty-four hours later, I'm walking home from a movie when it suddenly hits me so hard I stop walking, I stop and stare down at the sidewalk, my mouth gaping, my breathing stopped. I lean against a storefront window and tell myself to breathe.

"Oh... my... God." I say it out loud. I'm half-standing, half-sitting on a window ledge, alone. My hand is clutching my face, I'm keening like a mourner and I don't give a damn who sees me or hears me or what they think about me doing it. I have just heard the voice of God, the voice of my angels, the truth of my soul shouting out at me.

"I have nothing to be ashamed of... It's my *shame*, my shame is ready to die. That part of me that I have always carried, that part of me that felt like it was *my* fault, it was all my fault that I was molested as a child. The child that has been blamed ever since for not fighting back, not telling someone. That five-year-old has lived inside of me all this time and now, finally, she is ready to die. She is finally ready to die."

I have nothing to be ashamed of, I am not afraid anymore of who knows the truth about my life, that my lover is in prison; that I'm waiting out here, alone, for him to come home. I'll tell them all, I'll tell everyone at work, everyone who knows me and *I will not feel shame.*

And suddenly, there standing in the street I know that this is the release, this is the courage that I was waiting for, this is the moment of truth that has been pushing upward, bending my heart and my head 'til it bursts, breaks open and bleeds this beautiful, exquisite, holy water of compassion. My heart has broken open and revealed it's core to me and it is not full of shame. It is full of courage. I am not ashamed. I am courageous. I am strong and a hero and I am *not ashamed.*

SEPTEMBER *23, 19*__

Dear Mum, Dad, L__ & J__, A__ & D___, S___, E___, M___ and D____:

> *This is a very difficult letter to write. I wish it felt more like a relief*
> *than an awful thing that I don't want to do. But I have made the decision*
> *that it is more important to me to be true to myself and completely*
> *myself no matter what, than it is to be accepted, even by my family.*
> *I have been carrying a very burdensome secret that it is time I share*

with you. I don't expect any of you to understand and I am not asking for understanding or compassion or help of any kind. I just must be true to myself and in order to do so I can't go on lying about who I am and what my life is really about.

I can't even find the words to say this. There aren't any good words or words that make it seem not so bad.

I wouldn't have lied about it for so long if I hadn't been worried that it would mean the end of being part of the family. As much as you all may think that being part of this family doesn't mean anything to me, that's not true, although it means more to me to live my life as I want to than it does to be part of anything. But rejection is painful at any time in life.

Anyway, here is the secret. M. is out of town but not for the reasons I have been telling you. He's in prison. He will be there for another year at least, possibly longer. When he gets out, I plan to marry him and I'm truly sorry if that upsets you and makes you feel ashamed to be related to me. Whatever you think of me for standing by him in this, I have searched my soul for months, since he was arrested, and I know that being with M., honouring the genuine love and friendship that has grown through many hardships and trials, is the way that my heart needs to go. In spite of everything, M. and I truly respect each other in a way that I don't think is common to find in life. And no matter what it means in the way of sacrificing certain things, I still want to spend the rest of my life with him.

He didn't hurt anyone or do anything that I see as so terrible, although I know all of you will think that breaking any law that gets you in prison is pretty terrible. What it was, was stupid and desperate. I make absolutely no excuses for him and have said all of this to him, that I don't in any way think that it was okay for him to do what he did. And neither does he.

But I do understand how he got there and in spite of his stupidity in doing it, I believe I could have done it myself if I had been pushed to my limit. Again, I make no excuses for him but the truth is that he was on so many prescription drugs for his back injury (this was true and his arrest happened about two weeks after his surgery), and he was in so much pain all the time that I know his thinking was completely screwed up and he figured it may have been cancer anyway and he just didn't care anymore. None of this is a reason or an excuse or anything like that. I just would hope that if you care to look at some of the circumstances, maybe you wouldn't judge him—or me—so harshly.

Anyway, the bottom line is, why I'm telling you all this is because when everyone called for my birthday, it really sickened me to lie about my life. I am alone all the time, but not because he's working out of town. I am alone because I have chosen to be so until I could make the decision of whether or not I would wait for him and stand by him. Most of the time I have felt that I would stand by him but of course there have been many doubts and many fears about the future, which I have had to face and to discuss at great length with him. My decision was never mindless or blind love. It has been very deliberate and carefully thought out and my decision to stay with him is firm.

We weren't allowed to see each other face to face for a long time, but I have been visiting him in prison since it happened. Now that he is in a penitentiary, we are allowed day-long visits, and there's no glass between us. We just sit at tables in a big cafeteria and compared to the horrible places we used to visit in, it's almost normal. Prison life is not what the press makes it out to be—not at ALL. What you read in the newspaper about how prisoners eat steak and are treated like kings is total, absolute fabrication. Prison really is hell and prisoners are treated like less than human. The guards make their extra money by bringing in drugs that they sell to the prisoners (drug addicts are sick people to be pitied), which keeps them under control. Prisons are terribly corrupt and the public will never hear about it because if you speak up then you will be punished. I have learned to just put up with how they treat you, even as a visitor, because otherwise they'll just add time to his sentence and make it harder on both of us.

I have joined a support group that helps people who get out of prison to stay out, and get on their feet again. So many of them really want to go straight but they are either weak, or because they don't know any other life than the life of a criminal, they end up committing crimes again and end up back in jail. Most of their crimes aren't against anyone but themselves and the vast majority of the criminals in Canadian jails are in there because they are drug addicts. These people need psychiatrists and medical help, not prison cells. But instead of treating the problem where it starts, we build bigger, meaner jails and we think because we don't have to see them, they don't exist anymore.

And the newspapers will always report the isolated case of some guy who kills someone and gets off with two or three years because of a technicality but they never report the thousands of cases of young kids who could have straightened out their lives if they were just given the right help and guidance. They never tell you about the guards who literally get away with murder because some guy they beat to death (because he was black or because he reported their illegal activities or just for fun) has no family or his family is too poor to fight it.

We spend $60,000 a year on each prisoner—paying lazy fat-ass ignorant guards who sit around and watch T.V. all day—instead of putting that money to better use trying to educate some of the ones that are worth saving. By no means am I saying this is most of them, but not all the people in jails are horrible and vicious and disgusting. Some of them are and I don't have an answer for what to do with them. I think killing someone should have a penalty of death but what human being has the right to say that another human being should die? Except the ones that commit the unspeakable crimes, what other thing should be done with them except to rid society of them completely? I just don't have an answer for all of this, only that I know that not all these guys are completely immoral or bad or worthless.

Anyway, I have learned a lot about the subject of prison and crime, something I never in a million years thought I would have any reason to learn about. And I think that of all things, the justice system should at least be cleaned up and should be just, although I don't know whether that's possible because there's so many people in power making so much money from having people in prison. But the more I learn about it, the more I believe that it is an issue worth educating people on, and so I have gone off on a tangent a bit to tell you some of the things I have learned from this experience.

Anyway, none of this changes the fact of what I am telling you. And that no matter what your choice is—whether you reject me for this or not—I am choosing to stay with M. and be true to myself. I can't hide the truth of my life to my family and maintain self-respect.

I have explained M's crime to A. and J. from the beginning—I cannot lie to my own children. I have let them make their own decision about how they feel about what he did and have answered all of their questions honestly. A. has been with me to visit M. a few times and although he knows that what M. did was very wrong and very stupid, he still loves M. and recognizes that he is a good person. J. doesn't seem to have formulated much of an opinion either way, but it has been a very good lesson for him and I don't worry as much about J. getting into trouble now that he has seen first-hand what happens when you get caught.

I won't be telling anyone connected with my job because I believe that's completely different. Work is separate from the rest of my life, separate from who I truly am. I am not ashamed to wear a mask at work and allow them to think I have a very normal, perfect life. But with my family and friends, it's different. If I can't be myself, honestly myself, then my whole life is a lie, because nothing is as important to me as honesty. Ironic, that I choose to live with a convicted criminal because I value honesty. But it's even more ironic that M. is without a doubt the most honest person I have ever known in my life, in spite of his crime.

I have tried to answer any questions that I thought you might have so that you would get the whole story at once. I'm not sure if I really want to talk about this to any of you, or even if any of you will still speak to me after you've read this. Either way, what I do not want is any pretending. I don't want to avoid the subject or to act like this didn't happen, or we just won't talk about it. I am not ashamed to have made the choices I have made and I am not ashamed to be who I am. But if you can't take this in and need to just walk away from me, I won't hold it against any of you. That's really the truth.

And no matter what, this experience and the soul searching it

*demanded of me has taught me more about myself and life and the real
values I want to uphold in life than anything I could have dreamed up
for myself. As much as I would never have chosen this lesson for myself,
I am so grateful for all the truths I have learned and the strength,
courage and wisdom I have gained. I know, you probably all think there's
no wisdom in me staying in this, and you probably think I'm making a
very foolish mistake. I will stop trying to convince you otherwise. After
all, you could be right. In any case, I am who I am.*

From W's Journal

SEPTEMBER 28, 19__

The Hero Learns the Difference between Dignity and Pride:

PRIDE is the sin of Eden

SHAME is the sin of being human; the price of being human:
>VULNERABILITY at the hands of an "inferior"—(less evolved human)
>BEING AT THE MERCY OF an "inferior"

DIGNITY versus PRIDE—Learn the difference between Dignity and Pride

DIGNITY—The Hero learns dignity even in the face of seeming failure:

The Dragon Wins. The Maiden, the Hero's Beloved becomes dinner.
The Hero is defeated.
BUT !...
Because the Hero maintains his Dignity he is spared. And he discovers that
his Beloved, the Maiden, has escaped unharmed.
THUS!...
When the Hero maintains his Dignity, the Beloved is safe. When the Hero
acts out of Pride, out of Ego, the Beloved is killed.

PRIDE is a merely human attribute and easily lost or damaged. DIGNITY is
an integral element of the soul and cannot be stolen from us.

❖

I sat at one of the little tables in the visit room, crushing stray bread crumbs with my index finger, brushing them away with my hand. An idle gesture carried out with the utmost deliberation.

> *The countdown had been pared away, at first a week at a time*
> *time itself barely acknowledging its passing as it slinked away past us*
> *Through slivers of days we waited, feeling each day peel away beneath us;*
> *pithy hours were breathed through until*
> *at last*
> *now holding taut the whispers of minutes*
> *we watch*
> *we wait*
> *the last moist wedge of time scrapes past under the impatient blade of our*
> *anticipation*

The search coming in had been much less intrusive than I had expected. I hadn't dared bring anything that might give them an excuse to send me home—no jewellery, no valuables, no nail polish, not even perfume, I didn't know if it couldn't somehow be manipulated into contraband—the inmates were ingenious with such things. The guards were enormously more gracious than usual, treating me as a human being, a real person, almost like themselves. I was suddenly just a wife wanting to be with her husband and there was even a shadow of compassion from them as they opened each jar of cream and inspected the contents of both toothpaste tube and shampoo bottle. All was in order.

I listened to their instructions intently and followed them to the letter. My leather knapsack was replaced by the institutional blue duffel bag and as directed, I carefully placed all of my belongings into the new bag, leaving my own behind in the search room. That had answered my question of how they were able to keep people from smuggling drugs inside the linings of bags, etc. And yet, with all their precautions, the smuggling still ran rampant, prisoners and their visitors applying surprising brilliance to come up with ever more ingenious methods of moving contraband through, into and around the institution, right under the twitching noses of the C.S.C. hounds.

I waited, as instructed, for the other wives and mothers while their bags and belongings were checked and transferred. My manicured nails tapped lightly on the table, no crumbs left to play with, my fingertips restlessly sniffed the shiny lacquered surface for distractions.

I stretched out my fingers, clenched, stretched them again, examined the manicure—TAP, TAP, TAP—no, too noisy, too conspicuous, fingertips only, softly tap tap tap, silent, counting, breathing, counting, silently tapping.

I had prepared for this weekend like a wedding; shaved, plucked, preened, cleaned, polished, and dyed to perfection. He wouldn't even notice, I knew that, none of those things ever elicited as much as a blink of an eye from him.

"You're always perfect to me," he'd say, as sincere as it was sentimental.

"But what if I don't look as good as you remember me? What if you've only fantasized me into perfection and you look at me for real again and you all of a sudden realize I have gross ugly bulges and rolls and scars that you've forgotten?"

In recall, I see his head thrown back in laughter, he enjoys my unintended humour and then he looks at me, the laughter now pressed back behind the straight-lined smile that's only his, "Oh, God, Sweetie, that's exactly why I love you so much."

As enigmatic as he is, the statement will not be elaborated upon, there will be no further explanation, and I must simply accept it as truth.

But the butterflies in my stomach waltzed a little now, when I struck against the question once again. In spite of what he'd said, the sphinx's smile on his lips, the matter-of-factness of his always response—"Couldn't happen, Sweetie-pie. You're *always* perfect to me"—the panel of critics that occupied my mind remained unconvinced.

The guards walked us, women and children, wordless, to our "trailers," which actually turned out to be little housekeeping cottages, much like the ones up North that you can rent for summers by the lake and winter skiing. The only difference, at least the only one that mattered was that these cottages were each divided and surrounded by eight-foot steel fences, topped with three-foot extensions of barbed wire. Beyond the compound were the perimeter fences, wired to detect movement of any kind against them, and more barbed wire and beyond those were the exterior barbed wire fences that surrounded the entire collection of buildings and stretched the length and breadth of these many acres of prison property.

The inmates had already been deposited in their respective trailers, fences secured by locks and chains, before the visitors were brought around. The sound of metal scraping and clashing made the butterflies inside me leap nearly out of my throat. M. was standing on the front porch stoop wearing the leather baseball cap I had sent with his clothes and a boyish smile that betrayed his air of confidence. I smiled at knowing that his butterflies had awakened too.

I peered at him, still smiling, silently watching as the guard pulled the chain, rasping, through the gate and creaked it open while I stepped through onto the inside walkway. M. stepped towards me and took the duffel bag from my hand. He hugged me quickly, nervously, feeling conspicuous and shy and wanting to just get us behind the closed door of the cottage, at last to be alone. He took my hand, still awkward, and kissed my cheek and whispered, "Welcome to paradise," and we both laughed as we walked up the steps together, nervous as two sixteen-year-olds on a first date.

M. slammed the door shut on the world of the prison surrounding us. The boyish smile widened into an enormous wide-open grin and he grabbed me and held me tight as he could, and I didn't care that he almost squeezed the breath out of me, the hardness of it was good. He loosened his hold to look at me and he held my face in his hands. My own eyes traced the thin brown circle around the iris of his blue ones and I saw the fences and the guards and the barbed wire and the last fourteen months suddenly wash away in the flood of that blue iris sea. A last blissful, aching moment of anticipation and we clumsily kissed again. He pressed his lips full and soft on my mouth, the kisses we had wanted but hadn't dared to take in the visit room filled with the eyes of strangers were finally taken without apology.

M. pushed past my shy protests, my tears, my butterflies and his, coming up into our throats like a herd of elephants. My body bowed under his embrace and I bent nearly backwards away from him, stupidly terrified by the strangeness of a man's body. He kissed my neck and eased his arm away from behind my back. I straightened up, smoothed my hair away from my face and forced my eyes to the floor, examined my shoes, his shoes, anything to avoid his eyes. Gently, he reached for my hand and pulled me over to the sofa where I sat beside him, legs tucked up underneath me, my body braced against the tidal wave of tears that threatened to break at any moment.

We sat not speaking; he stroked my hair and studied every inch of my face. I pressed my hand to my mouth, as though to lock my emotions safe inside me and still I avoided his eyes though I felt them gently sweep over me. I barely dared to breathe for fear of the tears as I sat wedged between my practised resistance of the past nineteen months and the strangeness of this new reality where suddenly another body was no longer foreign, forbidden to pierce my separateness.

The rasping of metal outside made me jump, and he soothed me with whispers, laughing softly at my nervousness and to cover his own. "It's okay," he instantly read my fear, "they aren't taking me away, Sweetie, they're just bringing our groceries." It seemed a simple enough concept, but it escaped me and I sat like a stone on the sofa alone while he went outside and brought in the groceries he'd ordered. I'd forgotten the mundane—I had deposited money in his account two weeks earlier to pay for our food. I watched as he brought in armloads of food—bread, eggs, tins of tuna, chicken, I sat dumbly watching him until he had brought everything in and set it all on the kitchen table.

"Well, Sweetie..." he waited, and the smile broke into a laugh.

I shook myself and stood up to help him put things away. It was the perfect distraction. We opened all the cupboards one after the other and announced what we found—"sugar, and look—there's all different buckets full of these little mustards and ketchups and everything... oh, here's some onions, they must be left from the last people... are you *sure* we have to throw away everything we don't eat... Positive... you're not supposed to leave anything... God, we'll never eat all this food in three days... yeah, but you can't get half loaves of bread or just a few eggs...." We shuffled and shoved and prodded every shelf and drawer until we were satisfied that we knew where everything could be put away and found again. Then I emptied all the dishes into the sink and soaked them in hot soapy water. The sheets were neatly folded in drawers but still I had to throw them all into the washing machine and watch invisible germs wash away under the gush of hot of soapy water.

The whirl of activity had grounded me. I sat out of breath on the sofa, my legs stretched out on the coffee table. He sat beside me, arm around my shoulder and kissed first my hands, then my temple, my ear. "Don't worry, Sweetie," he whispered, "I've waited this long, we can wait 'til you're ready." And I allowed my head to melt into the well of his shoulder. Somewhere between our first cup of coffee alone together, and our laughter at his stories of the antics of other inmates, I was almost ready. Ready enough to allow the first passionate kiss, the stroking of my bare skin as he slipped the sleeves of my dress down to elbows and off my arms; soft, fleshy kisses on bare skin, and finally the terrifying breaking of our long fast.

My jaw tightened, my face stretched itself into a Münchs' silent *Scream*, the tears begged to be released and I resisted all of it. My body and my mind were at war, the weapons of instinct and fear seized first by one and then the other, my physical resistance gaining ground in the battle. Until finally, my battered mind, exhausted by the terror of vulnerability, slowly began to give way, my will draining away like spent blood on the battlefield, in my mind the thin wail rising, "It's M., it's my M., I can do this."

We say good-bye
There are no tears
And though there's still so much to say
We both are silent
You take my hand
It's time to go
And in the night when I'm alone
I will remember

There are no dreams we haven't dreamed
That other lovers would have dreamed
There are no places in the heart
We haven't known
Haven't shown
It's time to go

(Bridge)

We say good-bye
There are no tears
And though there's still so much to say
We both are silent

The days resume much as they were before, I concentrate on work, on the boys, does the hallway need painting again, what will I make for dinner tonight.

I cook less often than I used to but when I do I enjoy it. And best of all I can afford the groceries now, complete with all the luscious gourmet treats that comfort me, remind me that I really have dragged us out of that pit of poverty.

I wash each mushroom, three different varieties I bought—why not, I can afford it. None of them are brown or mushy, I didn't buy them from the "reduced" pile, they are all perfect and I smile thinking how a mushroom can come to mean so much. It feels good to slice them, firm and exotic and knowing they cost me $4.95 a pound.

I throw them all into the butter melting in the pan, with the garlic cloves just going crystal. I'm smiling all the while, stirring mushrooms in the pan and thinking how much M. loves mushrooms and I say to myself, "When M. comes home, we'll eat mushrooms every day."

And that is how it is, every moment of every day. Behind every thought, every breath is "When M. comes home..." It has become a mantra. I don't even realize it anymore, I have to concentrate to hear my own thoughts say it, and then I catch myself, every hour, every moment comes the thought of him, of us, of how it will be when...

Like an organ-grinder pumping his music-box, I grind out the days of my life haltingly, raspy, a little at a time but never quite enough all at once, or smoothly enough to carry a tune.

Life must go on, they say and I know that it's true. I ache to think that every moment of my life is holding its breath as though waiting to be completed. My every thought is wrapped round with him, my every action has him somewhere in it, making it feel unfinished, an absence that can never be corrected. I live in incompleteness, each moment an intake of breath that's never released.

Life does go on, it is oblivious to me, to us, to anyone. The clock ticks on and that's my *life* I'm pushing along with it, pushing the hours and minutes ahead, rushing it along so I can finally take that one full breath, live that one complete moment again where I don't hear myself say, "When M. comes home...."

And then, suddenly, watching myself as if in a slow-motion movie-clip, I become a bystander as I grab the pan full of mushrooms and hurl it across the room. From somewhere outside myself, I hear the clang of the pan as it slams up against wall in the hallway. The sound of it feels penetrating and good, chipped paint and plaster in crumbs on the floor, I stand there watching as dark grease stains soak deep and streaming into the ivory of the wall. My arm is splashed with hot butter but I don't notice it burning my skin and later when I see the burn marks I can't think how they got there.

I clean up the mess of fried mushrooms and burnt butter and wipe down the grease from the wall enjoying the damage like a precocious child. I don't cry.

I say out loud, though no one is there, "I guess this wall will need painting after all."

OCTOBER 10, 19__

**To the Office of the Deputy Commissioner
of Correctional Service of Canada:**

My husband, M. R., is serving a seven-year sentence, commencing July 22, 19__.

Attached is a form he was provided while at Millhaven Assessment Unit, which shows September __, 19__ as his eligibility date for Unescorted Temporary Absence; May __, 19__ as his first eligibility date for Day Parole and November __, 19__ as his first eligibility date for Full Parole.

He arrived at Warkworth Institution November 19__. He was "assessed" in a three-minute interview, and was advised that he would be required to take the following programs: cognitive skills, substance abuse and anger management.

At that time M. was advised that he was number 180 on the eligibility list for his recommended programs, including the anger management program.

Six months ago (i.e., after about five months) he was advised that he was number 150 on the waiting list. He went to his Case Management Officer to enquire whether anything could be done to move him further ahead on the list, since he was very keen to take the anger

*management program **for his own sake**, in order to assist him in dealing with his day to day life in prison, and in order to establish and use
these skills before his release. His CMO advised that she would issue a
"PPRS" that would move him up on the list. He has been advised that
this was done at that time.*

*Last week he visited the program department again (he makes
regular visits to find out whether there is room on the program list to fit
him into any vacant spots) and was advised that he was now back to
number 177 on the list for the anger management program.*

*When he asked how he was moved back, he was advised that new
inmates who had shorter sentences were put in ahead of him, even though
their mandatory parole dates extended far beyond his first full parole date.*

*Because of the shorter sentences these offenders are serving, they are
not eligible, as he is, for early (day) parole and will have to serve the
mandatory two-thirds of their sentence before receiving a parole hearing.
In addition, these individuals (with two to four year sentences) are
required to take these programs; however, since their parole is not based
on their successful completion of these programs, they frequently "drop
out" of the program, leaving behind empty seats that could be filled by
others. Being aware of this fact has added to my husband's frustration.*

*M. has been advised by his CMO that due to his high score for
cognitive skills, and due to other factors involved with respect to the
substance abuse, he would probably be exempt from taking either of
these programs, although he has shown interest in taking the substance
abuse program from a personal development perspective. That leaves
only the anger management program as a certain and necessary requirement for his possible early (day) parole in May 19__. However, we will
not know for sure about any such exemptions until he meets with the
Program Delivery Officer.*

Our main question is as follows: **Why is he being bumped back
on the eligibility list when in fact he has a more urgent requirement for his programs and why is he not receiving appropriate
motivational support for taking these programs, thus assisting
him in his sincere efforts to prepare for reintegration into society
and resumption of a normal life?**

The Deputy Commissioner of Correctional Services of Canada has provided clear and supportive guidelines pointing toward the encouragement of earliest possible release for those offenders who have shown indications of being ready to reintegrate into the community, **prior to their mandatory release dates**.

From the Mission Statement of Correctional Service of Canada (not a precise quotation):

"The mission of Correctional Services Canada is to contribute to the protection of society by actively encouraging and assisting offenders to become law-abiding citizens, while exercising reasonable, safe, secure and humane control. An active motivation ideology is intended to encourage offenders actively and constantly to participate in programs designed to correct criminal behaviour and to improve [their] ability to deal with daily life situations."

From a speech by the Commissioner to Case Management Officers (not a precise quotation:)

"The Parole Board and the Service share a responsibility to ensure that offenders are released in a timely and appropriate manner.

"We should not be planning programs or doing case preparation with statutory [mandatory] release as the target date. Case preparation must be completed if offenders who have addressed their criminological factors adequately are to be released at parole eligibility.

"Clearly, this requires co-operation from the community in terms of information gathering, community assessments and release plans. If the risk at that point with the best programs and supervision available in the community cannot be contained, then we have to continue to work with the offender to reduce the risk prior to statutory release."

There was further commentary emphasizing the responsibility of Case Management Officers with respect to reintegration of offenders being more accurately (paraphrased)

"not to be focussed on the margin of error in making an incorrect decision by releasing an offender who may not be ready, but should be aimed at reducing the margin of error in not releasing an offender who is ready."

These are our immediate concerns:

1. We wish to have an *interview with the program delivery officer* to find out whether in fact all three programs recommended will be required, i.e., any exemptions.

2. We would like to be advised when we can expect *admission into the anger management program as well as the other programs if they are required.* Since it is our understanding that these programs take about twelve weeks (each) to complete, we are anxious to get started without further delay.

3. We would like to submit an *application for admission to Minimum Security, through the office of the Deputy Commissioner*, if possible. Our fear is that our actions in going direct to the Deputy Commissioner may result in retaliation, which would eliminate my husband's eligibility for Minimum Security and early parole. Thus far, M. has not had so much as a warning or write-up for inappropriate behaviour or failure to comply with any and all rules and regulations of every institution he has been in.

4. M. has submitted several job applications to no avail. He is anxious to be put to work and kept busy. He has always been a hard worker and finds the idle time contributes to his sense of frustration and feelings of hopelessness. My husband believes he has been "warehoused," forgotten by the system, swept under the invisible, but very present, carpet of indifference that exists in this system.

5. My husband is now eligible for an Unescorted Temporary Absence pass. He has already been permitted two Escorted Temporary Absences to attend Dr. J's office (an orthopaedic surgeon) and the hospital in Peterborough for tests. During those absences, his conduct has been that of a "model prisoner" as remarked by his attending guards.

*We wish to apply for an **Unescorted Temporary Absence pass for Christmas** of 19__. Warkworth Institution (visiting) is closed on Christmas Day and Boxing Day. Last year, we were unable to see each other for Christmas, a very lonely and discouraging experience for both of us.*

We respectfully request that consideration be given to grant a pass so that we may spend this Christmas together. My husband and I are very close and being apart last Christmas was a hardship on both of us. In addition, we have the support of a community support group specifically for offenders, ex-offenders and their families, "JustUs," that has been working with us since my husband's incarceration in the Toronto Jail.

The JustUs co-ordinator has volunteered both her support of our application as well as any assistance she may provide, i.e., personal supervision of the visit, etc. We are also supported in the community by clergy, our doctor, close friends and my husband's family (he has two sisters and two small children). We are confident that a T.A.P. for Christmas would be an opportunity to provide evidence of my husband's readiness and ability to reintegrate into the community at the earliest possible date.

I believe we may also call upon the support of the Community Assessment Officer Mr. P., who conducted an interview with me prior to the granting of our Private Family Visits. Mr. P. has indicated his opinion that, given the circumstances surrounding my husband's criminal act, M. is not likely to re-offend. Mr. P. has offered his moral support on a number of occasions.

According to the form provided to us, the decision for granting a T.A.P. resides with the Warden. Please advise how we may proceed, given our concerns with regard to pursuing this matter through the usual channels and possible negative repercussions that could ensue.

6. C.B., my husband's (former) Case Management Officer, advised that a psychological assessment could establish the fact that my husband is (1) by nature, non-violent (2) not likely to re-offend or to commit any future act of violence. He submitted a written request for a psychological assessment and was supported by his CMO with a "PPRS," over a month ago. He has just been advised by his new CMO (formerly an administrative assistant in the psychology dept.) that this could take up to six (6) months to be processed.

*We wish to have a **psychological assessment conducted as soon as possible** to ascertain whether conditions exist that would indicate my husband is/is not likely to re-offend. If the results of such an assessment indicate that he is not likely to commit future acts of violence, we wish to submit this as supporting documentation for an application to transfer to Minimum Security.*

M. and I would be grateful for any assistance we can obtain from the Deputy Commissioner's Office. We regret that we do not feel secure about the motivations of personnel responsible for dealing with my husband's case at the Unit level (Unit __, __ Block), and therefore have avoided addressing our concerns to the Warden's Office for fear of retaliation.

I can make myself available to speak with or meet with anyone at any time to pursue these matters further. You may contact me at home at (___) ___-___. My husband has also expressed his willingness to meet with a representative of your office personally, if necessary.

We sincerely thank you for your time and interest in our case.

Yours truly,
W. R.

I've been up since 5 a.m., getting ready for my 9 a.m. appointment with B.G., the Warden of Warkworth. The drive up there will be about two hours, fifteen minutes, but I give myself an extra half hour, to be absolutely sure I'm not late.

The letter I wrote to the Deputy Commissioner, Mr. O., got me in to see him at his office in Kingston a week ago. He was incredibly gracious, kind and unexpectedly compassionate. In the end, however, he had to advise me that in spite of the merit that he saw in our case, it really would be up to the Institution to deal with us through the proper channels.

"You understand, of course, Mr. O.," I told him, "that we have been trying for months to deal with our case through the appropriate channels."

I patiently reiterated the recent history of M's progress or, more accurately, lack of, to Mr. O.: our months of trying to get scheduled for programs that were prerequisite to temporary absence passes (days or weekends home), which were an absolute prerequisite for obtaining parole. With M's first parole date coming up in less than nine months from now, it was already impossible to get the all necessary programming completed in time to be eligible for either passes or parole. Even if he qualified for parole on every other count, he would sit behind bars another six months or even a year or two past his eligibility date before he would meet the programming requirements.

Like so many others, M. had been "shelved" by the system. After many letters to M.P.s and numerous requests to M's Case Management Officer, we finally identified what, or rather who, was behind the delays.

The Unit Manager of M's cell block was named Ms. H. Under the guise of "procedure," Ms. H. had established a method of warehousing inmates as though they were inventory. Rumour had it that years before, Ms. H. had fallen in love, once or perhaps several times, with prisoners who then used her influence and of course, dumped her when she was no longer useful to them. An unattractive woman to begin with, her bitterness hardened into an ugly shield and earned her the nickname, "Cruella De Vil" after the cartoon movie character from *101 Dalmatians*.

By the time we met up with her, Ms. H. was a lonely, bitter, middle-aged woman with the power to affect hundreds of inmates' lives... and the thousands more lives that broadened out in waves from each one, like the pebble dropped in a still pool. What could be more dangerous than a vengeful woman let loose in a system based on the power of the few?

Ms. H., in addition to her duties as Unit Manager, had positioned herself as chief advisor to the Warden. She was head of the Committee that reviewed all requests for programs, temporary passes, transfers to other institutions and applications for parole. She also trained all of the new Classification Officers, each of whom had a caseload of about ten to twenty inmates. As part of her campaign of tyranny, Ms. H. trained and instructed her staff, under threat of serious reprisal, to ignore, misinform and deny any and all requests by inmates.

Routinely, M. told me, men were told by the Classification Officers that they could not apply for parole, when in fact their parole dates had come and gone months before; they were told they were not eligible for temporary absence passes, a crucial requirement for obtaining parole; they were often refused even the most basic medical attention. It was well-known that passes from Warkworth were virtually unheard of, since all such applications eventually had to make their way across Ms. H.'s desk before going on to the Warden for approval. Inmates who tried too hard suffered dire consequences.

Of course programming, the system's biggest club next to parole, was routinely refused, denied and cancelled under Ms. H.'s absolute authority. Without such programming an inmate cannot satisfy a Parole Board that he is sufficiently "rehabilitated" to be permitted to rejoin society. Those without education, without families who would fight for them, were helpless. Even staff who had wanted to do the right thing, inmates reported, had learned to fear the backlash of disobeyed orders and instructions, right or wrong, when they came directly from Ms. H.

I held nothing back in relating these facts to Mr. O. and admitted that my information was based on "hearsay" from my husband and other inmates. The stories I had heard, however, were corroborated by other wives and family members. With so much at stake for M. and myself, I knew my argument was one-sided and personal. But without a voice courageous enough to speak that personal truth, and make it heard, make it known, then what hope did the others have, the ones who were too uneducated, too simple, too alone to speak up for themselves?

Mr. O. patiently heard me out, often nodding in agreement, allowing me to have my full say before he spoke. When I had finished, he paused a moment, considering all that I had said. He was exceedingly tactful in advising me.

"Mrs. R.," he began, his voice reaching me with a soothing sense of authority. Mr. O. was a well-groomed gentleman in his late fifties, dignified, white-haired, with the bearing of a soldier. He had long since left behind the every day vulgarity of Prison life. Now, he enjoyed the easy denouement of a long and successful career in the civil service, surrounded by the sumptuous gardens and plush décor that graced the historical building housing his offices.

But the glint in his eye as he heard my story told me there was spark in the old boy yet. He still welcomed a challenge. My short-skirted business suit didn't hurt, either.

"I understand that there may be some ...er ...resistance on the part of Staff to ...er ...carry out their duties as they have been charged to do. People are people and you know [he was disarmingly frank], well, we are civil servants. We don't like change and we don't like to be told to do things any differently than they have always been done."

"But we're only asking that established Correctional Services Policy be followed, it's all written down, is that too much to...."

"Yes, yes, of course. You're right. But policy is policy. It's there as a guideline only. We need to rely on our staff to implement it, and therefore, it's open to their ...er ...interpretation. Now, if I were to go over Ms. H.'s head to the Warden, Mr. G., I am sure that the repercussions, as you have already pointed out yourself, could result in ...er ...well, quite the opposite effect from what you are trying to accomplish."

Translation: If you go over the Unit Manager's head to her boss the Warden, she will fuck you but good. And damn straight, she can.

Mr. O. thanked me for my honesty, promising to make a call to the

Warden with a subtle suggestion that perhaps our case, and the standard procedures being followed at Warkworth, warranted some review.

I left his office with more hope than I'd dared to have in months.

The next day I received a call from Ms. H. herself, advising me that an appointment with the Warden had been scheduled, in a week's time, at 9 a.m. sharp.

I thanked her and asked, politely, trying to be neither timid nor demanding, "And it is Mr. G., the Warden that I will be meeting with?"

Her controlled voice masked an almost-exhaled sigh of exasperation, "Yes, that is what you requested, Mrs. R?"

"Oh yes, yes it is. And thank-you again. Thank you very much."

Bitch. The receiver was still in my hand, long minutes after the peremptory click on the other end. Oh, god, my heart sank. It's what we've been asking for since August, a meeting with the Warden. But hell, am I really ready for this?

I'm still asking myself the same question a week later, as I quickly shower and dress in the lifting veil of this post-dawn October 31st morning.

The trip seems quicker than usual and going against rush hour traffic, out of the city, I'm almost there with forty minutes to spare. I stop at the donut shop on the edge of the highway turnoff and kill off another twenty minutes. The drive up the country highway to the institution is beautiful, and I take my time. I breathe in the freshness of damp leaves, tilled fields and acres of drying corn; farmers fields full of baled hay roll down alongside each side of the road. Here and there along the road are welcoming witches cut out of cardboard; sheeted ghosts and jolly jack-o-lanterns are set out at the end of long country drives. Shrines to modern ghosts and goblins. I smile to think of the hallowe'eners who will be at my door tonight, decked out as angels and avengers. I relish the everydayness of the rest of my life.

I arrive at Warkworth, at 8:45 a.m. precisely, fifteen minutes ahead of my scheduled appointment. When I go to the intake desk, I am mistaken for an inmate's lawyer, in my most corporate blue suit, with the shiny brass buttons. I politely advise that no, I am not a lawyer. My name is W.R. and I have an appointment with Mr. G.

I am asked no further questions. She smiles and immediately calls the Warden's office to announce my arrival.

Thirty minutes later, I am still waiting. There are no chairs in the intake area and I pace quietly, trying to quell my impatience and rising panic. Maybe it was all a trick. Maybe there is no meeting. Maybe... my thoughts are finally interrupted by the clang of steel as the barred gate that separates this intake area from the outer corridor of the Prison administrative offices draws aside and a woman steps out from behind it.

The woman is wearing running shoes, stretchy black tights and an over-sized lavender sweatshirt, appliquéd with snowflakes across the front of it. She approaches me and introduces herself as Ms. A., M's Classification Officer. She somehow manages to entirely avoid meeting my eyes while she gestures me to follow her, leaving my outstretched hand decidedly unshook. She does not take me through to the hallway leading to the offices, from which she has just come, but instead leads me through to the same visiting area where M. and I have been having our weekend visits. There are two small glassed-in interview rooms off to one side and she points me into one.

"Have a seat," she instructs, still not ever looking directly at me. There is no mention made of my having waited a half-hour past the appointed time. I shake myself for expecting to be treated as though this were a professional organization, as though I had any right to expect even courtesy from these people. After all, I was the enemy.

I steel myself for the battle I can already smell.

It is small surprise to me when Ms. A. returns, accompanied by M., and announces expressionless, "We'll get started when Ms. H. gets back. She's busy at the moment."

"And the Warden?"

Her sudden smile is a bellowing echo of every condescending word, every superior look down the nose of every guard and official I have encountered since the first day at the doors of the Don Jail.

"The Warden?" and now she can't suppress a subtle sneer of amusement. "The Warden wouldn't be coming here." Her pointed finger tapping the table makes the last sound heard in the room for a few minutes.

M. and I barely breathe. My anger has risen like a tide up the back of my neck and it is everything I can do to stay seated and keep myself from reaching across the table and slapping the sneer right off her face.

Two years later I will recall this moment with some amusement when I read of this same Ms. A. being reprimanded for carrying on a scandalous affair with an inmate, ten years younger than herself. The newspaper reports how she and her convict lover were "exposed" and how both had admitted to having sex during almost daily "interviews" in her office. The newspaper article quotes her as stating, with emphatic defiance, "We are in love. I don't care what happens. I love him and I don't regret what I have done." We never read of the outcome, but we assume that since the reported reprimand is an extended leave of absence for Ms. A., with full pay, her "punishment" was likely little more than a transfer to another institution. Or perhaps nothing at all. The inmate, however, probably had at least a few months tacked onto his sentence.

Ms. A. shuffles papers in the file in front of her and taps her pen, distractedly, against her leg. M. has already told me a little about Ms. A. She is new to the job, it's a promotion for her. A month ago she was an administrative assistant in the psychology department of the institution. She has no background in social services nor any other correctional service credentials. She has no degree of any kind. And for the past month she has been making decisions, guided by her supervisor Ms. H., that affect the very lives, their entire lives for the rest of their lives, of more than a dozen men under her authority. I marvel at the power of circumstance. The power of absolute might. It requires no logic and no justification.

Ms. H. finally arrives and closes the door of the tiny room behind her. She hesitates a moment before returning a limp hand to my firm grip. She seats herself beside Ms. A. and folds her hands on the table in front of her.

"Well, Mrs. R.," with a dismissive nod in M's direction, "shall we begin?" Ms. H. asserts her obvious authority.

I notice that everything about this woman is pinched and pointed. I immediately recognize the uncanny resemblance to the Cruella De Vil character and if not for my anger at this moment, I may have burst into laughter. She is dressed slightly more appropriately than Ms. A., in straight black slacks and a white shirt buttoned up tightly against a thin, long, chicken neck. Her eyes, shifting and bird-like, lurk behind heavily made up lids that emerge blue and sharp from beneath shaggy eyebrows that had once been fashionable. Her chalky-white face is framed by wisps of grey-black hair, with more grey-black tufts combed over in little mounds across the top of her head. The hairs are cropped short in an attempt to conceal their sparseness.

I look evenly at Ms. H. and, keeping my voice calm, I ask again about the Warden.

Ms. H. and her trainee exchange a glance, a silent sigh of bored exasperation. "No, the Warden is a very busy man. He is not scheduled for this meeting."

"But you told me on the phone…."

"Mrs. R.," her tone annihilates further argument, "do you wish to meet with Ms. A. and myself regarding your husband's case… or don't you?"

Again, the power of absolute authority thrown in my face like a glove and I must swallow hard to keep from walking out of the room in disgust.

"Well, it is unfortunate that I was led to believe that my husband and I would be meeting with the Warden." I keep my voice even, firm and deliberate and ignore her eyes when she rolls them, "However, I am sure, Ms. H., that you will be able to refer to the matter to him for his review after this meeting."

Their expression of contempt is unconcealed. M., seated beside me, can feel the heat of my anger and I feel his arm land softly on the back of my chair. He is uncertain whether I will be able to contain myself through this interview and rightly so. I know I must steady my emotions if I am to win anything today. I set my square jaw like a rudder, determined to get through this without an angry outburst.

I open my file and M. and I begin to detail point by point, our requests, as addressed in my letter to the Deputy Commissioner. Their comments to each point are as shocking in their glib delivery as in their content.

We begin by asking when M. may expect to start programs. M. briefly recaps the history of his "progress" on the waiting list, from number 180 to number 177, in the past year.

"Mr. R., you are only one of 660 inmates in this prison, all of whom are waiting, some much longer than yourself, for programs. We've already told you, you'll have to wait your turn like everyone else.

"When new inmates arrive, whose mandatory release dates are earlier than yours, you will be moved back on the list, regardless of whether your parole eligibility comes up sooner than that of the new inmates. There is no way of preventing this, it's how the system works. This has also been explained to you previously."

Neither of them is aware that M's day parole eligibility date is less than nine months away. Neither seems the least bit altered in their opinion of how they should proceed, based on this new information.

"We do not even consider the day parole date, we look only at the statutory release date. All of our programming recommendations and decisions will be based upon the statutory release date."

No comment is made when I point out the fact that this is contradictory to the stated mandate contained in the Mission Statement of Corrections Canada. I assume that neither of them has read the Mission Statement.

"We will absolutely NOT commit to any kind of time frame whatsoever for you to meet with the Program Delivery Officer, or for commencing programs.

We ask about the status of our application for a Temporary Absence Pass (T.A.P.) for Christmas. Three weeks before, on October 6th, M. had taken his application to Ms. A., who immediately advised him to withdraw the application. She claimed he had left it too late to be processed in time for Christmas.

M. refused to withdraw the application. A week later, Ms. A. called him into her office once again and demanded that he withdraw his application. She did not recommend changing it to a later date to allow more time for processing, but insisted that the application must be withdrawn. He was creating an awful lot of work for a lot of people for nothing.

"We have already advised you, M. to withdraw your application. Since a T.A.P. requires a community assessment, which can take up to 60 days, it is futile to submit your application at this late date."

No reason was given for the fact that his application had now been sitting on Ms. A's desk for almost four weeks, half of the time needed for the processing to be carried out. His application was not completed by Ms. A. until after our meeting that day, guaranteeing that it would not be processed in time for Christmas.

"Ms. A. has completed a progress summary, however, to delegate authority for the decision of granting a pass to the Warden rather than having to go through the Parole Board. This is the first step in obtaining a pass."

There was stony silence when I asked why time had been spent in granting authority to the Warden, when in fact, the nature of M's offence, his sentence and the assessment form we had received already confirmed that the Warden was automatically given decision-making authority for any of M's passes. There had never been any need to apply to the Parole Board for M. to be granted a T.A.P.

We asked Ms. A. why the Progress Summary she had prepared was almost identical to the initial intake assessment already carried out at Millhaven. We asked why she had never interviewed my husband with respect to the details of the crime before having committed to paper such an important document.

"Well, I have read M's file and am comfortable in relying on the facts already presented by other interviewers."

We began to point out numerous discrepancies and obvious errors that could be supported by documentation I had brought with me. They were not interested in discussing any discrepancies or inaccuracies. That should have been taken up at the time of the original document (which we had only just received). The document would stand as is, permanently on file.

"In any case, Mr. R.," Ms. H. cracked her only smile of the meeting thus far, "if we take this version and your version, I think it's safe to say that the truth must lie somewhere in the middle."

I thought for sure M. would stand up and grab the woman by the throat and shake the few tufts of hair left on her head right out by their roots. Instead, he breathed in deep and slow. I waited for him to speak.

"No, Ms. H. The fact is, my version is the truth. And I can prove it. I do think I know the details much more thoroughly and accurately than the officer who spent less than five minutes questioning me before writing that report. I think it worthy to note, Ms. H., that in fact, I have insisted all along that I acted alone in the first two robberies, something that, if anything, will be counted against me. This is not corroborated by the writer of the first report, nor by Ms. A's report."

"Well, then Mr. R., I would say that we have done you a service in presenting you in a better light, and you had better cease your objections to this report immediately or it may go against you."

She made no pretence in her threat. It was direct, unveiled and witnessed. It simply did not matter. We were powerless, and she knew it.

"I already told your husband," the rising confidence in Ms. A's voice was obvious, as the battle now was clearly won, "that in order to recommend him for entry into programs, ahead of the others, I might add, or to recommend him for a T.A.P., it is critical that he demonstrate to me that he is ready. I don't know you, M. I have only been here a month."

I cannot contain myself and M. grabs my arm to hold me in my chair, "But that's not his fault! What about the months he has spent with his previous C.O., who by the way did "get to know him" and wrote several glowing reports about his demonstrated...."

"Mr. R's previous C.O. is no longer employed in my department." Ms. H. steps in swiftly to put an end to this discussion. "No," she replied to M's question, "she cannot be consulted. If you," boring beady eyes into M's skull, "were worthy of her confidence, then you should have no trouble convincing Ms. A. of the same." Her words are as clipped and final as circumcision.

We were shaken but not beaten. Not yet. We asked again about programming, about how we could help M. to qualify so that he would at least start his programs before his parole date.

"You need to give me something to work with," Ms. A. stated, adopting a slightly more conciliatory tone, now that the battle was securely won. "You don't seem to be able to account for how you spend your time at this point. You should be working if you are not in programs."

M. was so uncharacteristically patient with this latest assault that I swelled with admiration for him. "I believe," he spoke patiently, respectfully, not a hint of condescension in his voice, "that I have already explained to you that I have been trying, desperately, since arriving at this institution, to get hired on. The answer is always the same: there's a hundred guys ahead of you. I have submitted my resume, and was told that with my construction background, I would be taking a job away from a contracted employee, which would violate the contract that C.S.C. has with this outside construction company. And yet, I work almost for free, and the people they've hired, who do not have my fifteen years experience in construction, are being paid upwards of $30.00 an hour, under contract.

"As you also are aware, I am now volunteering in the Laundry, with no actual job there, just in the hope that I will be there at the right moment to get hired on when someone leaves. There is not one single department in this institution that has not been hounded by me for a job."

Ms. H. blinks her eyes, indifferent. "What about handicrafts? Or school? You could be spending your time at least, constructively."

Again, M. is so patient, so controlled I almost don't recognize him. "Ms. H., with all due respect, I have applied for numerous courses and I am told that only high-school courses are available in this institution. My scores on all the tests grade me at a post-secondary education level and quite frankly, the one course I did take provided me with absolutely no improvement of my skills or knowledge. It only served to increase my sense of boredom and uselessness.

"As for handicrafts, it takes money to buy materials, and they're not cheap. My wife has enough on her plate without having to supply me with materials to make things to occupy my time. If I had a job, however, I would then earn some money to buy my own materials. We are back to the basics—the chicken and the egg."

The metaphor appears lost on them both.

I break the momentary silence with the next item on our list. "What is the status of M's application for a transfer to a Minimum Security institution?"

Ms. H's reaction is subtle but unmistakable. She is so practised at hiding the emotions that move her, drive her unerringly toward her mark. But I see the flash in her eye before she clutches it back, pushes it back behind her absolute control. I have committed the cardinal sin. I have mentioned the unmentionable. And for this, I will be made to pay.

"Transfer?" she asks, the nostrils of her long, pinched nose only just flaring, almost imperceptible.

M. reminds her of his application for "Camp," also submitted on October 6th.

Ms. H. turns to look at Ms. A., who wriggles a moment in her seat before responding. "Uh, yes. I believe... that application was passed on to your C.R.X., Mr. P. He is supposed to complete his report within 30 days. If he does it, then it will go to Ms. H. for review."

"Supposed to... if he does it... these are not words that inspire confidence." I have now definitively crossed the line of what an inmate's wife may say to a C.S.C. employee, clearly her superior. I drive on. "What about accountability? Is there no one to ensure that Mr. P. does what he is paid to do?"

They are now both exasperated and have tired of the cat and mouse game. It's time for the kill. Ms. H. squeezes her eyes into a squint. Her voice is low and menacing, the words forced out between clenched teeth. "Well, maybe he will and maybe he won't. I work for Correctional Services Canada, NOT for you. OUR jobs are secure whether we do what we're supposed to do or spend our time picking our noses and filing our nails. Is that clear enough for you?"

The mask is off and so are the gloves.

"Or fornicating with inmates?" I hear the words but don't know whose mouth they came from. I turn to see M's ashen face and realize the words are mine.

Her smile is slow and evil, her teeth wet with saliva, the taste of the kill is already in her mouth. "Only the lucky ones," she spits out at me.

In spite of my outburst and the subsequent abrupt termination of our interview, M. is ushered through the motions of a case review. Within days of our meeting, he is scheduled for an appointment with the contracted Psychologist, for a psychological assessment to determined the likelihood of an escape attempt if he were granted a T.A.P.

The assessment is extremely positive and we are both ecstatic when we receive our copy. Except for the psychologist's comment that M. appears to rely rather heavily on the support of his spouse, which at times, M. admits, has caused some friction with some of the staff, there seems little in the report that can be construed as negative.

We are even more excited when we read the review by Mr. P., although it has not yet passed Ms. H.'s approval and so may never actually be committed to file. But Mr. P., who has been working with M. for the past several months, gives M. a copy of the original report, advising him, "Look, this may not be worth the paper it's written on, but I'm recommending you for a T.A.P. Keep this copy in case it gets changed somewhere along the way. I mean, it has to pass the Committee (meaning Ms. H.), and, well, I don't get much say after that."

Ms. H.'s pared down version of Mr. P.'s report reduces the recommendation from positive to without any serious or known negatives. Her comments on the psychological report are crafty and devastating. She is well practised at getting what she wants and from a six-page document that whole-heartedly supports M's application for a T.A.P. for Christmas, she manages to pluck out and crystallize the one vague comment that may be construed as negative and she even finds another. The psychologist comments that, while M. appears to take responsibility for his crimes, he appears to minimize somewhat, the impact and his own motivations. Ms. H. brilliantly ties this comment in with her own, "the over-bearing influence of the subject's wife and her seeming absolute control over his actions. Mr. R. does not seem able to think for himself, nor to make reasonable and rational choices without the input of his wife."

But I have been as tireless behind the scenes as she and my motivation is fuelled by love rather than hatred. I am determined to do all that can be done to have M. home for Christmas, and if we fail at that, then the consolation prize will be a move to Minimum Security. Although I know that Ms. H. will not release her inventory, not even one, without a fight to the death, I must try until I fail.

After the meeting, before even leaving the Prison Grounds, I make a call to the Deputy Commissioner and relate to him the results of our meeting. I leave out nothing, including being tricked into thinking we would be meeting with the Warden and my final outburst that put an immediate end to the interview. He couldn't suppress a chuckle at my final comment, but chided me just the same for losing control. He spoke to me as an indulgent father would speak to a precocious child, "I have heard that it happens, but you know, you just can't come right out and say it. You are something, Mrs. R." Mr. O. appreciates forthrightness, a quality that I know I possess in great measure. And the feisty sparks that go with it.

Mr. O's assistant calls me two days later to advise that a meeting is scheduled for M. and myself with the Warden in two weeks. For real this time.

We are both terrified when the day comes. So much history has already gone into this meeting, I don't know whether to begin by apologizing or to come out swinging.

Ms. H. is in the Warden's office when I arrive. M. is still being summoned from the range. Ms. H. does not acknowledge me, though we are seated in the same reception area, until after the Warden's secretary asks if I have met Ms. H. She acknowledges that yes, we have met and my heart falls to my feet when I realize that she will be present at this interview.

M. arrives and we wait together in a small reception area reserved for inmates. He is not invited into the Warden's office until the Warden is ready to see us.

Mr. G. is a huge man with a stern face and knowing eyes. His warmth is unmistakable and I imagine him bouncing baby grandchildren on his knee in the life he lives outside his official duties.

Ms. H. is mute almost through the entire interview, perched demurely on the edge of the sofa in Mr. G's office, looking for all the world like a meek and mild, butter-wouldn't-melt-in-her-mouth, conscientious and earnest civil servant. I am nauseated by the spectacle of her sweet smiles for the Warden and her rehearsed familiarity with the details of M's case. I call her on several lies, though I am tactful enough this time to simply say, "Oh, excuse me, Ms. H., perhaps you will recall that it was actually... [this way or that way, or whatever was the truth behind her lie]. And I had documentation to prove my points.

The Warden pares the interview down to three questions directed at M., one at me. He asks M. why he did it, where the money went and what he plans to do with his time if the T.A.P. is granted. He asks me only, "Did he tell you about the robberies before he committed them? Did you know what was going on?" I was so surprised by the question that I blurted out, honestly, "N-no. I mean, I guess... he lied to me."

The interview is over and I am in tears before I get to my car. Lied to me. Lied to me?! How could I say that, how could I tell him that he lied to me and that he should get out on a pass?!!

M. phones me at home that night and we talk about it until the phones are cut off. M. thinks I said the right thing, "I mean, it's obvious I deceived you and he knows that. He just wanted to see if you'd tell the truth. And you did. I think he would respect that. I mean it, I think you said the right thing." M.

tries to comfort me. The tears burst out fresh again as soon as I heard his voice. God, I longed for him to just hold me and tell me everything would be okay. For now, I had to content myself with only his voice, coming from a hundred miles away.

There was nothing to do now but wait. The Warden had requested that Ms. H. have her recommendations on his desk by December 2nd.

She submits her report on December 4th, one day after Mr. G. has been transferred to another institution. The report is reviewed by the Deputy Warden, Mr. K., who is left in charge until a new Warden is appointed. The Deputy Warden has never spoken to M., never met me, never reviewed the case.

I am crushed, but still determined. After several messages to Mr. K., the Deputy Warden, he calls me on December 7th. He patiently hears me out on everything that has occurred since last August. He agrees to review the file and call me back.

Mr. K. is as good as his word and calls me back the next day. He assures me that he has thoroughly reviewed the file and has discussed the case at length with the Unit Manager, Ms. H. He has accepted Ms. H's recommendation that the T.A.P. is not a manageable risk at this time. However, he will be reviewing the file further for recommendation for a transfer to Minimum Security. He assures me that it appears that there is a very good chance that my husband will be considered for transfer, shortly after Christmas.

I am still clutching the receiver ten minutes after Mr. K. has hung up. She won. They won. No matter anyway, who won, who lost, the fact of the matter is we spend another Christmas apart. And we were so certain last year that it would be the last.

I come back from the dining room after a dinner of turkey and dressing of sorts, the only decent meal all year, it's a dry straw to grasp in this hellish place. Every phone on the range has been busy all day, a line-up even, fights and arguments, I stay well out of it. It was smart to phone W. when I could, yesterday morning.

She said she'd be with friends tonight anyway, the boys are having Christmas with their dad's family. What did she say she was going to do—carolling, that was it, go carolling at the old folk's homes, at least brighten someone's day. Her smile could brighten anyone's. It sure would brighten mine.

I'm lying on my bunk imagining the smell of her and sound of her and softness of her hair. Like a bucket of ice water thrown at me, I hear the familiar throaty voice of Ms. H. in the corridor outside my cell. Small surprise she's working tonight, no friends or family that could stomach spending Christmas with her. So she inflicts herself on us and double pay to do it. A captive audience, more like captive amusement, monkeys in a zoo is how she sees us. And god, you gotta know there is no greater joy in her cold witch's heart tonight than to see us miserable sons-a-bitches feeling lonely and forgotten.

She's come to find me, opens the door to my cell of course, without a knock. I pretend to be asleep. She steps right up to my bunk and, sensing her about to shake my shoulder, I suddenly jump up and back before her bony hand reaches me. The thought of her touching me makes the turkey in my stomach roll over.

She stands there, silent, looking up at me, an expectancy around her steely eyes. I sit silent also, my legs hanging off the edge of the upper bunk. I meet her stare full bore and we square off, each of us knowing just how deep and terrible runs our mutual hatred.

Slowly, a sideways smile begins to pull her thin lips upward in an evil-looking curl. She has become a full caricature of herself, an evil wicked woman with evil wicked wishes and evil wicked ways of making them come true. She turns her back on me to leave, and then, at the door of my cell, in a quiet, raspy drawl dragged oozingly through tight teeth, she turns to me and says, "Merry Christmas, R."

Christmas alone again, I thought the last had been the last but....

I watch snow arrive again and scold myself for self-indulgent sadness... it is alive, this time, a moment. It is life to be with loved ones and children and life still even without him in it, standing there in front of me at turkey dinner. It is life still and the days beat by and I will not come again by this place in time.

Come outside your nest of loneliness
Come find the fun of friends and song

Come to sing old bones to sleep a Christmas ballad
Christmas sweet as some they think they have recall

Kind friends, good friends, sweet and lonely all we are again this year. We go to stir the old ones from forgottenness. I pull my coat around and close and scan the ochre bland and oatmeal grey with few fresh flakes to snow white the burnt crust of week ago winter. Is it Christmas yet, is it yet?

The old ones some of them so hopeful still, rich lives lived full of children is it? Then why are they alone tonight, enlivened by the grace of carollers doing duty, our lonely lives come brighter at the sight of ones more pitiable still than us. And clapping purpled shrivelled hands, dry smell of old decaying skin though washed a hundred times you smell them dying in your sight.

Then to Yonge Street, just to stem the dying tide and feel the City beating there, watch the alone others who dream only of warm beds and food to eat, I sitting in my car and warm and fearful they are me.

I step out into snowflakes, sidewalks—crowded lonely people
Gays and prostitutes
Homeless—they scare me, they stink and rotted teeth are begging. They have
*   nothing, needy, hypodermic stuck in your arm they will suck the life of you*
they are lepers
they are angels
they are the ones we were taught to love in starched white shirts and pleated
*   skirts and proper shoes, they taught that we must*
look after the little ones
of god
they are the unsheltered
the pitiable the wretched
they are the useless the forgotten the hated
they are spurned and ridiculous
they are jokes against themselves
they are fearsome they are fearful
they wander soulless days searching lost
they are without hope
they are whirlpools suck you under
they are sinking sand deserts of despair
they feed on each others weaknesses, cannibalizing failures
they are prisoners they are free men
they are horrible they are beautiful

Return to warm and shelter if alone at least it's not on beds of concrete cold, good night for beggars with guilt abundant. I light the candles keeping vigil spanning hours 'til the day is over, night is past and this is lived and over. Thank god, it will be different next year.

Yes?

Chapter Fifteen

Março 18, 19__

Dear M.,

Haven't written in so long, I thought I'd put a few of my thoughts
down on paper for you.

I had planned to write today, but instead I got into reading some of
my old journals and I'm struck by a few things. Mostly by how hard I
have always tried to "get my lessons" and how difficult they always seem
to be. And also how much love has always meant to me.

I guess I am an incurable romantic, but I can see in reading through
it all, it's not just the fantasy of the white knight, it's not some foolish
addiction to the idea of being in love. There is a sense of destiny, of a
CALLING to love greatly, immensely. All through it is a thread that there
is a sense to it all, a pattern and cohesiveness. In spite of all the struggles
and splits we had, I think I knew that you and I were meant to be
together and to be apart was totally against the order of things.

Yet, being apart in the way we are now is what has made us so
strong, so certain that coming through this will be the testing and the
MAKING of our love. The fire.

This is what I wrote, years ago, when you and I had split (I thought,
for good):

"The longing is so intense it's unbearable. There is nothing,
NOTHING I wouldn't do or suffer to have this love that I long for. Surely
I could not have such a longing without a reason, without an end to it. It

is so intense, so profound. It's not like anything else I have ever felt or read about or heard someone tell me. It is PROFOUND LONGING.

"It's not simple loneliness, it's nothing like loneliness or the neediness of wanting to be with someone. I know that feeling well and I recognize it when it comes upon me. This is very different. It is so CORE, it is a feeling that my sole purpose in coming into this life was to fulfil some pact or agreement, as though the fate of all relationships for all men and women for all time will be shaped by THIS one.

"God it sounds so stupid, maudlin, so teenage. But I feel it to the absolute core of my being—the longing for an equal, one who is not afraid, one who has the courage to go in, to dig deep, to be there in all the hurt and grief and heal it, come through it all with me.

"If my soul has ever spoken to me, it is speaking to me now. I came here, to this life, to accomplish this, to create such a love. It will be unconditional. It will change everything forever. The longing must be fulfilled."

Reading that now, I guess it sounds like I was off the deep end or something. But there is such absolute conviction in it, an awareness when I wrote it that even though it sounded nuts, it was truly my soul speaking to me. Do you think, I mean, really it must be so, that if two people, say you and me, really work through all kinds of shit to simply hang in and be there for each other, to love each other unconditionally, as I feel we are trying to do (though I know we fall very far short of the ideal), it would HAVE to have an energetic influence on everything, everyone, because everything is connected. All is one, it's the first lesson of spirituality no matter what religion or philosophy one espouses.

So if all is one, then one—or two—can affect it all. And perhaps then, it was my soul reaching out to me and pushing me toward creating this energetic "adjustment" to the Universe with you. I hate to dismiss something that I expressed with such passion, knowing it sounded crazy, but knowing also that I was speaking of things beyond our normal comprehension. There are some truths for which we must simply suspend disbelief, if we are ever to get the lesson.

I found another little excerpt I want to share with you, from about ten years ago, when I had just left K. and was on my own for the first time in my life. I was having so much trouble just getting through all the fear of being alone, going back to work after being home with the kids for so long. It was a very tough but a very growing time. Anyway, there was always so much to get through, the self-doubt, the fears and failures and... blah blah blah. But listen to this, it's so wise, even in the midst of all that, and before I had started reading so much and actively "therapizing" myself. I wrote this to myself:

"The stone's been rolling, growing it may still fall and crush you—chances are it will and what will you do then?

"You will crawl out from under it, dig out from under it and you'll be disappointed to find you are still alive. And maybe they will have to scrape the pieces together and put you in a box and file you under 'mentally unfit' in a nice, clean, white room.

"But maybe not. Maybe you'll find that the parts that are crushed beyond repair are the ones that held you prisoner."

Now that really was insightful coming from where I was at the time I wrote that bit. God, I really do feel everything so intensely, passionately. I've got to remember that and give myself a break and a reminder when I fall into these immense valleys of emotion and despair. As I read back in these journals, I have been "going through" something for the last fifteen years. It's been one mountain to climb after another, and I have always panicked in the darkness of the experience. I've written over and over again, "I have to stop running away from the blackness—stop panicking, stop railing against it, and ALLOW it to overcome me, experience it. I must face the blackness and realize that I can and will live through it and not go crazy."

So much has changed and so much has stayed the same. I will always be passionate. I will always feel everything intensely. There's not something wrong with me for feeling things the way I do, the only thing is, I really have to learn how to manage this high level of sensitivity so that it doesn't cause me so much heartache.

I think I am slowly learning.

See you soon, Love, W.

May 10, 19__
Dear M.,

Wrote a little something you might like. It's to be part of the novel I started a couple of years ago (that I'm still working on), but clearly the influence of my present life is going to change the path this novel is taking. Read on:

"Justice is not simply a matter of opinion," I said.

"Oh?" Anthony piped up. He had been sitting silent, seemingly a detached observer to the conversation. Apparently he had a view on the subject himself.

I felt I was up to the challenge.

"Terri, you are so very intelligent that it surprises me that you have not seen that rigidity prevents one from achieving the very insights that your highly developed soul is presenting for your further evolution." His directness in addressing me so personally took me by surprise for a moment and I wondered if he was being a patronizing boor.

But I saw the sincerity in his eyes and knew that he was simply expressing the truth of his personal observations, or at least what he saw as truth.

"I don't think that my opinions are rigid, Anthony. I only think that if you believe in something then you should think that your belief is right, or else why have it? Call that being rigid if you want to, but some ideals like justice or love get played around with so much that instead of coming to some balance between what's black and what's white, people end up just being wishy-washy. They only think they have an opinion but what they really have is a so-called 'belief system' that can be swayed by the wind. I think what you see in me as 'rigidity' is actually steadfastness to what I believe to be true."

"Very well-spoken Terri, but I feel that in your admirable desire to be true to yourself, you deprive yourself of a wider scope and thereby perhaps lose the kernel of truth you so deserve to know."

Throughout this conversation Anthony never appeared to be lecturing me or putting me down, so in spite of the fact that he was calling me to task amongst a group of several people, I didn't feel any sense of defensiveness. I felt I was hearing truth. And I wanted to hear more.

"Shall I tell you a little story, that I might illustrate my point?" he asked.

As always, his very formal manner of speaking made us giggle a little, but he took no offence.

"Oh, yes, Anthony dah-ling," Janine mimicked with drawling British affectation, "Do go on my deah." The slight tension that had begun to arise dispersed immediately and we all laughed.

Anthony smiled, impressing me again with his ability to sincerely join in and laugh at himself, since he knew he was an unusual character to say the least. He patiently waited until the snickers had subsided, and then adopting a theatrical but totally compelling tone of voice, he began telling us this story:

"This is a story of a love affair that spanned not a lifetime but many lifetimes. Exactly how many lifetimes isn't known and doesn't matter. In this story we hear of only two of them.

"The souls involved were incarnated as a man and a woman, the same each time. In the earlier of the two lifetimes, the woman had been a young Italian maid. She was unmarried, poor but very dignified of bearing and pure in spirit. She was what one would call humbly noble. She was a hard worker who enjoyed her simple life and needed few friends, in fact took little interest in other people at all.

"At the end of the second world war a former Officer of Hitler's army came to live at the inn where the young woman worked. The war had taken a toll on him. He looked much older than his actual age, and even to one who had never before met him, he appeared as a shadow of his former self, a walking ghost. He spoke very quietly and in fact, very little and kept to himself always.

"For endless hours he would sit quietly at the window of the inn overlooking the street, never speaking a word, seldom nodding acknowledgement to anyone who passed by.

"As part of her duties, the maid tended the garden that extended from the front window out to the street. For many hours she would work in the garden while the man sat quietly watching her. At first only shy, hesitating glances were exchanged that eventually led to polite nods, then smiles and the two became friends.

"Friendship soon grew into passionate love, in spite of the German officer's complete and open confession to the young woman of his terrible past: many innocent people had suffered and died at his hand; he knowingly gave orders for the annihilation of many innocent prisoners of war. At the end of the war, a supreme act of forgiveness on the part of one of the prison camp survivors whose life he had uncharacteristically spared, allowed him to escape. He avoided facing charges for his crimes by fleeing to Italy and abandoning his identity.

"However, the supreme irony of having been forgiven and released changed the Officer forever and in fact left his spirit broken with guilt and remorse from which his human ego had no desire to redeem itself. He resolved within himself to pay for his crimes through self-denial and remorse for as long as he lived. His spirit could not overcome the burden of his guilt and shame and thus, he became a ghost that lived only to punish himself with the daily remembrance of his heinous past.

"Strange as it is, as love will always be, the young woman saw in him a nobility of character worthy of redemption. She being young and more impetuous wanted to marry the German, but in spite of loving her passionately, and knowing that being a respectable girl he could only have her affections through marriage, he refused her. The crimes of his past left him feeling completely unworthy of her love.

"The tragedy was of course, that the man died alone, still racked with guilt and the horrifying memories of his crimes. Instead of reclaiming his soul through love, for which his higher self had allowed the young woman to enter his life, he chose to die unredeemed. The young woman, unable to heal her broken heart, died shortly afterwards. She never loved another.

"That was not however, the end of the story. For the pair had obviously not completed the task of attaining love, the highest of all ideals, which their souls had been reaching towards. It took another lifetime to accomplish that goal.

"The second time the man and woman were together, they each remained male and female respectively. At the time they met, she was older and more mature, having been married before and now raising two children alone. He was a young man of high ideals but absolutely no means, having been raised himself by a struggling single mother.

"As a boy he had run wild, his behaviour unchecked by his mother whose hardships in raising her three children alone were almost too much for her. With no parental guidance to steer him away from indulging in his passion for mischief, his bad behaviour gave way early to a young life of petty crime.

"The boy was eventually caught by the authorities and sent to prison. From there emerged a young man determined to have a life of which he could be proud, a life without poverty or need or the complete absence of love that he had endured in prison.

"And now it was that he met again the love of his former life. The two were immediately attracted, neither one at that time suspecting they had already been in love with each other before. Before long they decided to make a life together. Sadly, they suffered many hardships as they attempted to build a life together, since money was forever in short supply. Both worked hard, but nevertheless serious financial woes eventually overtook them and they separated.

"But true love never dies and the young man was determined that he would be with the woman he loved and worthy of her love. He believed that since hard work had amounted to nothing, his only choice was to return to a life of crime, and thereby achieve his goal.

"And so he did. And did so with tremendous success because he not only dragged himself from out of his own financial quagmire, but also helped all those around him, family, friends, colleagues and many of the poor and homeless as well. And in spite of the seeming immorality of his acts he was scrupulous in ensuring everyone's safety and in fact preyed only on the purses and pocketbooks of those whose wealth was exceeded only by their greed and stinginess.

"The young man returned to his love with pockets full, able finally to dissolve the only obstacle to their happiness together and the two, as the saying goes, lived happily ever after. And their happiness, of course, was increased tenfold as it spilled over to everyone they had contact with throughout that lifetime they shared together.

"So by the strangest twist of justice," he finished, "resolution was reached for two souls and love, being the highest of all ideals, was served." He folded his hands in front of him, like the drawing of a curtain on a stage.

"And the moral of the story is," I said when he had finished, "justice can come clothed as its antithesis."

"My dear," he was not being at all condescending, "Justice IS its antithesis. It is above morality. Justice is not judgement, which is black and white. You cannot define ideals such as justice or love or happiness. The moral to the story is, perspective is everything."

I looked in his eyes and felt I understood his message. And although I couldn't completely agree I couldn't disagree either. Without a doubt the sincerity with which he expressed his philosophy left no doubt that he was speaking his truth—an absolute truth he had come to know through much living. If only for that, I respected him and what he had to say.

In the following days we travelled over long stretches of quiet countryside. Anthony entertained us with his stories of adventure in India or Italy, or the coast of South Africa. It was impossible to dislike him, or to keep from being fascinated by his point of view, always somewhere just a little off-centre. Or, as he would probably say, having a point of view would mean that one hadn't yet reached the centre from which all perspectives are clearly seen and opinion becomes non-existent. "In order to have an opinion," Anthony said, "one must have a point of view, from which point one sees circumstances, events or people from a single perspective. But by attaining the centre of that same circumstance or event one is able to see all perspectives simultaneously and with equal clarity.

"In the case of people seeing other people, one must first attain one's own centre in order to see all perspectives of another. And having attained the centre where one can clearly view all perspectives, how does one then say they have a 'point of view,' for they in fact have all points of view and having that vantage site they would then know that to sacrifice this greater all-encompassing vision in order to adopt a view from a single point, would be sheer stupidity."

"Anthony, I would have to say, you have a point, there." I said, then quickly turned to look at him, a sly grin escaping, "or should I say, you have a most all-encompassing vision on that subject."

We all laughed, Anthony enjoying being the "jokee" every bit as much as the joker.

I don't know if it was simply the more time we spent with him the more he made sense, or if he actually saved some of his more profound and erudite arguments until he had broken us in a little. But I found myself beginning to question the firmness of my own beliefs, which I had thought so unalterable. Was it possible Anthony was having an influence on me?

On looking back, I believe that Anthony himself didn't actually believe all of the arguments he put out but presented them strictly as a manner of teaching. He had certainly become a teacher for me, having an undeniable gift to gently prod my thoughts until they gave up their real truth.

One such argument was most disturbing in that it was so sound and yet so seemingly immoral at the same time. But I was left shaken by my own inability to refute it.

We had just finished a lively discussion about reincarnation. It surprised me to hear all four of us agreeing that it had to be true. Even Janine with her scathing sceptic's eye said that she didn't doubt that it was true but questioned my viewpoint that the life one comes into has nothing to do with one's previous lives.

"Well, I don't mean it has *nothing* to do with your past lives," I clarified. "I just mean, I don't believe that if you are a mean and stingy person in this life you will come back as a someone who has to live in a ghetto or something. I mean, it can't be as simple as that."

"I believe you are both right," our wise companion interjected. "Terri is most correct in saying that 'karma' as you people like to call it, isn't as simple as 'tit for tat.' It's not so much that 'what you do comes back to you' (another of your charming North American expressions), as it is a matter of getting the lessons at whatever price.

"Of course, one's soul will always prefer to choose the gentle approach, and if one has had many lifetimes in which to learn from one's mistakes, then the soul can achieve most excellent results

with the very gentlest prodding. If however, one stubbornly refuses
to learn the lessons that the higher self has already mapped out for
itself, then the methods of teaching must necessarily become
harsher.

"Take for instance, the case of the murderer and the victim.
Given the choice, which would you rather be born as, the child
who grows up to be a man or woman who takes a life, or the one
who has his or her life taken from them?"

A silence while we pondered this. I honestly couldn't choose.

"Well," Roberto ventured "I guess it is better to be the one who
got the lesson."

"Exactly!" Anthony enthused, delighted at Roberto's response.

"It really doesn't matter which one you are, since both chose as
souls to adopt their particular human lives, with all its misfortunes.
And hopefully, in spite of the apparent tragedy, both got their
lessons from it."

I shook my head, "No, Anthony, I'm sorry, that's just too pat
an answer for me. There simply IS no justice in murder. I mean
self-defence is one thing, but you said a 'murderer.'"

"Yes, I did, and you are right in pointing out that I did NOT
mean a justifiable killing, I meant MURDER."

"Yeah, well if I had to become a murderer to get a lesson, then
thanks but no thanks." I said, feeling sick at the thought.

"Aha, so there is your choice, you would rather be the victim."
Anthony was getting livelier and I knew he was getting warmed
up for another insightful discourse.

Janine interjected dryly, "God, I wouldn't want to be the victim,
either. Can't I just be the fly on the wall that gets the lesson by
observation?"

We all chuckled a little. We could always count on Janine for
comic relief.

"Unfortunately, my dear Janine, there are few souls evolved
enough to get their lessons simply by observation. But perhaps
those who are, do reincarnate as flies on the wall."

We all laughed again.

"Jokes aside, Anthony." Roberto picked up the thread of the lesson.
"Do you think that the life of a murderer is worthy in some way?"

"But of course, Roberto. If it were not so, then there would be no murderers. And no victims. Look, let me draw it for you in this way. Let's say this fellow is not a murderer, but he's a good-for-nothing rogue who beats his wife. The wife, on the other hand, has been raised by a mother whose husband beat her, and whose mother before her had also lived a hellish life of constant abuse.

"The victim then, the wife, is trapped by the legacy of wretchedness from which she came and because of inherited guilt and a life steeped in low self-esteem, she can see no escape. She then raises her daughter who observes all of this and so the cycle is perpetuated, one generation after another.

"In fact, since human cells actually retain memory, it begs the question whether in fact the fourth or fifth or sixth generation victims of this world, having been bred in an environment soaked with fear and self-loathing, are in fact genetically altered in some fantastic (but entirely plausible) Darwinian twist of fate? So that by now, abuse has become RIGHT to them both in body and in mind."

"Whoa, wait a minute there, Anthony," I objected, "Now you're jumping way off into something else and I'm still back at choosing between becoming a loathsome wife-beater or his equally loathsome wife."

"THANK-YOU!" Anthony shouted with such enthusiasm that it startled Roberto and he nearly drove us into a farmer's field.

"Hey, you guys, this philosophy is getting dangerous. I'd like to carry on with this life for a little while longer if you don't mind," Roberto warned us, laughing.

"So sorry, Roberto. I DO get carried away sometimes. But Terri's response is *exactly* what I was needing in order to make my point."

"Glad to oblige, Anthony. What did I say that was so profound?"

"You said, 'loathsome wife' and therein you have made a judgement that this person is to be held responsible in some way for having become a victim."

I thought about it for awhile and was shocked to find that he was right. Where was my sense of compassion for this poor woman? I expressed my thoughts out loud.

"Don't be too hard on yourself, Terri. You are not

uncompassionate for seeing the wife as responsible for her circumstances. For we are all ultimately responsible in that we have choices available to us that our *soul* always reveals to us but that we can choose to turn away from. Sometimes leaving behind all that one knows, regardless of how horrible it is, is more frightening than stepping into the light where you know nothing of where you are going or how to get there. Trusting the light is a tremendously difficult challenge and many of us humans turn away from it, leaving our souls most frustrated, I am sure."

"Okay, okay," Janine spoke up. "So, yes I see that because she's an adult, and yes maybe there are supportive elements and agencies and everything out there that she could turn to if she had the courage and all that. Okay. She's an adult and altered genes or not, she ultimately chooses to stay.

"But what about the kids? They are innocent victims. They stand by and see all this and they have no way out, they have no voice. God, some of them are babies when the abuse starts. And they don't even get a chance to develop any self-esteem with which to make a choice, right?"

"Exactly right, Janine," Anthony responded. "Only the child's mother can rescue both herself and her child from such a life. It is up to her and her alone to reach for the divine help that is always provided, though sometimes difficult to see. For the soul never gives lessons without giving also the tools with which to attain them. Which brings us right back to where we started, would you rather be the victimizer or the victim? The victim is the one with the greatest motivation and therefore the greatest power to change the situation. In grasping what may seem like bare threads of hope the victim may be able to put an end to this abhorrent cycle."

"And the murderer? Has he any power to change his fate?" I asked.

"Undoubtedly," Anthony answered. "But judging by your reactions, it would seem to me that the soul who chooses to become the murderer may have made the greatest sacrifice of all."

I was left without a response.

Chapter Sixteen

*J*UNE *2, 19 —*
Dear M.,

I just watched (again) part of the movie "The Bridges of Madison County." You haven't seen it. I saw it the first time two years ago while we were split up and you were out West. I really loved it then, it was a huge hit with everybody, 'cause it's this exquisitely sad love story. And it's supposedly based on a true story, which makes everyone believe it could happen to them, this little sliver of greatness called Romantic Love could even happen to them, ordinary people. In the end, the two lovers never get to be together because the woman (Meryl Streep) chooses her family's dignity and respect over her own happiness. So she and her lover (Clint Eastwood) have only the memories of the four beautiful days they had together and then they both go back to living sad and loveless lives. Well, her life isn't loveless because she loves her children, but her whole life is about duty and doing what is best for everyone else, and on and on.

Of course, seeing the movie again especially the part where she tells him she's not going to run away with him, in the light of what we are now going through, I couldn't help feeling really awed by the largeness and at the same time, everydayness of what we're doing. Romance is so ordinary. Our dreams are so ordinary, our desires and longings and hopes for the future are so utterly simple, they are everyone else's too. We are the "Everylovers," and like Everyman we embody the whole vision of what it means to be human and, in our case, to love someone deeply and completely and to use the word we've both used—perfectly.

But when is love ever ordinary? If love lives forever, if love is the only thing that endures beyond this earthly life, then how can this enormous love between us, this bond that stretches over and under and around everything that goes on in our very ordinary lives, be anything but extraordinary?

Our love IS extraordinary and that is the definition of love— everyday experience that explodes the limp myth of the heroine and her lover riding off into the sunset. Real love, real romance is much too brilliant a light to be entombed in a single, unalterable, picture-perfect fantasy. It lives side by side with the inane. It is seen only in half-light and the world's greatest poets have not been able to create a satisfactory metaphor to describe it perfectly.

Because to know it, it has to be lived, there is no telling of what it is. So now I'm completely at a loss for words because other than to pull out my paints and splash this page with every colour and its variations and every shade and shadow and subtlety that's ever been imagined, it cannot be committed to paper.

Love, W.

Rain starts heavy and full, fat drops like thumbprints hurl themselves against the windshield. I seem to be driving for hours, I'm numb behind the steering wheel, I don't hear the road rolling away underneath the tires for the longest two hours I've driven until I am there at last.

I step out of the car and pull my coat around me. The rain has stopped but the drops still hang lazily from the overhead hydro lines. A drop splashes bold on my head as I cross underneath them. I feel its coolness spreading like a star on the centre of my scalp. I reach up to rub it away but change my mind, it's a blessing, it's my tears given back to me, the river I've cried.

There are papers to sign, no doubt, I'm to meet him at room number twelve. The gate grinds away in front of me and I pass through, another fat drop letting go its grip of the barbed wire overhead, it splashes on the bridge of my nose, another grazes my eyelash. I reach up to flick it away and find real tears there, fresh ones, they're warm not cool.

I take the steps a little slowly, not hesitation, but reverence. This is a moment I will play many times, many lifetimes, slow-motion and quick, play it over and over in my mind, it must be memorized precisely. I count the steps as I take them slowly—one, two, three four. I open the door, the glass is still tinted and behind, the grey uniforms blurred, like the rain washed them blurry and watercolour sheer. Grey watercolour sheer they're washing away before I can speak.

I move to what should be the counter, but it's blurring out of sight and there's no book to sign, where has the book ... got to be? Now my eyes are closed tight against the washing away people and I feel myself stumble... my eyes... I can't open them, I can't see, I must open my eyes and trying as hard as I can I'm thinking the tears have glued them shut, I can never open these eyes again, the rain, the tears, my eyes are closed forever.

I wake up.

I'm barely breathing, my breath held like a knot high up in my throat. I let it out, slowly and carefully, blowing it through my mouth like a shield, performing a ritual of holding, waiting, it quells the panic. The next breath will come now, naturally, I won't have to wait for it and wonder if it's there. I am breathing. Slowly. And blowing it out of my mouth until I feel the panic subside. I dare not move until I'm sure it has passed. I am breathing. The breath is coming without effort. I am blowing it all away without effort. I was dreaming.

My heart is pounding less loudly now and I find the courage to roll, ever so slowly, onto my side. I mustn't let the night see me move until I am certain that I am safely away from the broken blister of the dream I have escaped. I gingerly pull at the duvet, tugging it ever so secretly under my chin, as though to move too suddenly or deliberately will cause the dark to devour me even as the last drying drops of the dream cling behind my open eyes.

Tomorrow I will make the drive for the last time. Tomorrow I bring him home. I've been crying for days, for a week in fact. It's not really happening, I find myself saying in the broad awake daylight, even as the last days scrape away, loosening like a snake's skin. I hold the skin up to the light in the night when I wake from my dreams and shiver underneath the duvet, the skin on my arms cool and dry like the snake's when he's shed all the days we've been waiting.

I review the instructions again, for the hundredth time, mentally checking that all the paperwork is signed, everything submitted as instructed. They will release him, just as they've said, I won't be turned away at the gate and the washed away watercolour guards were only a dream. He's coming home. My life is about to take up where I left it, like a clock on a shelf, that's finally been taken down and wound back up again. There's life in the old clock still. There's life. I have my life... back.

The organ-grinder is grinning, relieved to grind out a whole tune at last.

I let my eyelids close softly, still quiet. A warm tear has settled in the hollow of the bridge of my nose. Outside it's raining.

Organizations that helped W. and M.

Rittenhouse, founded in 1990, is an agency dedicated to bringing transformative justice instead of retributive justice to our criminal justice system. Transformative justice simply means making the basic goal of a criminal justice system healing, not revenge. Rittenhouse believes that crime can become an opportunity to bring transformation into the lives of victims, offenders and their families.

Rittenhouse
157 Carleton St, Suite 202
Toronto ON
M5A 2K3
Canada
Co-ordinator Giselle Dias

Phone (416) 972-9992
Fax (416) 923-8742
www.interlog.com/~ritten

JustUs is a non-profit organization that sponsors support groups both in the community and in institutions, including weekly support groups for both ex-prisoners and for family members of prisoners.

Just Us
c/o Emmanuel-Howard Park United Church
214 Wright Avenue
Toronto, Ontario
M5R 1L3
Canada
Co-ordinator Maria Karajovanova

Phone (416) 534-9133
Fax (416) 534-3355

Also of Interest from Canadian Scholars' Press

STORIES OF TRANSFORMATIVE JUSTICE
By Ruth Morris

Ruth Morris is one of the world's leading spokespersons on penal abolition and transformative justice. In this book, she outlines why the current adversarial system of justice fails victims, offenders, their families and ultimately society as a whole. Citing stories from Canada, the U.S., New Zealand, Australia, and around the world, Morris demonstrates that there is another path to follow that would transform misery victimization and punishment into new opportunities for healing and understanding. This is an inspirational work that proves that turning the other cheek unleashes the power of transformation.

$19.95   paperback 6x9   ISBN: 1-55130-174-1   Published May 2000

THE CASE FOR PENAL ABOLITION
Edited by Gord West and Ruth Morris

The Case for Penal Abolition marshals convincing arguments from a number of scholars and activists for abolishing not only imprisonment, but overhauling our entire penal injustice system. The movement for penal abolition is as old as prisons themselves, which from their beginning have failed to achieve any of their stated objectives—individual and general deterrence, rehabilitation, and restoring a sense of justice. Both street crime and corporate crime are considered, acknowledging that corporate crime causes more damage and death than recognized criminals do.

The Case for Penal Abolition challenges us all to move away from failing penal systems towards a new democratic global humanity in resolving human conflicts and legal issues.

$19.95   Paperback 6x9   ISBN 1-55130-147-4   Published May 2000

PENAL ABOLITION: THE PRACTICAL CHOICE
By Ruth Morris

Most people would agree that the criminal justice system does not satisfy our society's growing needs. Despite this dissatisfaction, the criminal justice system continues to grow into what is universally recognized as a failure. Morris believes that if society is to find its way out of this predicament, we must focus on these key questions: What's wrong with the system we have? Why is it still in place? What do we want instead? How do we get there? In a concise style this text answers these questions citing evidence and giving examples. This book is an excellent addition to the criminologist's library.

$14.95   Paperback 6x9   ISBN 1-55130-078-8   Published 1995